WANDERINGS ALONG THE RIVER WANSBECK

from Fourlaws to Cambois

T H Rowland

First published in 1995 by Northumberland County Library,
The Willows, Morpeth, Northumberland NE61 1TA

Printed by Pattinson and Sons, Newcastle upon Tyne

British Library Cataloguing-in-Publication data

A catalogue record for this book is available from the British Library

ISBN 1 874020 12 4

Cover Illustration: Map of Northumberland by
Lieutenant Andrew Armstrong, 1769

CONTENTS

LIST OF ILLUSTRATIONS

ACKNOWLEDGEMENTS

I have to thank Northumberland County Library for assistance, especially David Bonser and Lesley Kelly. My wife was companion for the travel involved and typed the original script. The photographs are my own except for the aerial photographs for which I have to thank Professor Norman McCord and Newcastle University. Northumberland County Record Office provided information.

This book is dedicated to the memory of the Reverend John Hodgson, Vicar of Kirkwhelpington 1823-1834, Vicar of Hartburn 1834-1845, born 4 November 1779 – died 12 June 1845.

I am particularly pleased that it should be published in this year which sees the 150th anniversary of his death.

T H Rowland

INTRODUCTION

A river as a route is different from a road. A road tries to get somewhere direct-ly, even though it may wander. By contrast a river only goes directly when it is in spate, cutting new channels and carrying things away with its waters.

The River Wansbeck has been notorious for its flooding, but usually it mean-ders in its normal progress. The river is the better theme for the traveller. Can the journey not be much more interesting than the destination?

The river starts on high ground among the hills and mosses. It varies seasonally with its supply of water, and on the surface it can be made stationary in the form of ice. The Wansbeck is not the proper name of our river. Northumberland streams are called "burns", and "becks" are found in areas of Viking settlement as in Yorkshire and Cumbria. Old maps and writers give the name of Wanspeke or Wanspike, and there is a variety of spellings for it. The pike is said to refer to tim-ber raft or bridge over the marshy waters. An old map gives the mouth of the river as Wansbeach.

To find the sources of the river you have to travel to Fourlaws Head on the Roman road called Dere Street and now numbered A68. It was the main route to Scotland and today it is busy with heavy traffic. Yet the area is remote and habita-tions are few. The land is mainly rough grazing and it has always been sheep coun-try. In medieval times Dere Street was used as a boundary line on Fylton Moor. To the west were the lands of Hexham Abbey and to the east were those of the Abbey of Newminster (Morpeth). Tyne waters went to the west and Wansbeck waters to the east. The monks had farmsteads called granges and because of Scottish raiders, they needed defensive towers. The pastures were "summer grazing" and the sheep would be moved for the winter. In those times many animals were killed and salted down for winter meat, since there was little food for them until spring returned.

The River Wansbeck traverses in turn the territory of three local councils – Tynedale, Castle Morpeth and Wansbeck. The Tynedale area comes as far as Kirkwhelpington, and to explore it you can take a field road to Three Farms, Plashetts, North Heugh and Carrycoats. The A68 is reached at Cowden, where once stood a toll house. The road continues North by the Tone Inn at a very undu-lating progress and Waterfalls, a remote farm, is seen on the right, near the cross-roads at Fourlaws. Here another narrow lane goes to the right – eastwards, and the sources of the Wansbeck are to the north of it. The infant river passes under the road to Sweethope Loughs and winds its way to Kirkwhelpington. The road reach-es a junction near Ferneyrigg – one way goes East to Kirkwhelpington; we take the other which follows the route of the disused railway towards West Woodburn. The Wanney crags rise in menacing fashion to the west, now partly screened by conifer plantations. There are remains of old mine workings at Stiddle Hill with an airshaft still showing and an opencast site on the other side of the road. Then the Ridsdale Ironworks can be seen on the A68, which we take and return to Fourlaws, getting

magnificent views of the countryside on the way.

The Fourlaws crossroads is a suitable place to stay and survey the landscape. Westwards can be seen Walltown Crags on the Roman Wall, and the land nearer slopes towards the River Rede and Bellingham.

Fourlaws Farm on the A68, which goes to the right. The Roman Road, Dere Street and camp are to the left.

Near to the Roman road (A68) on the left and before Fourlaws Farm is a Roman marching camp called "Swine Hill". It is roughly rectangular and has inturned entrances for defence. Such sites were used by the Romans who built the road, and their camps were also used on route marches. Romans travelled regularly into Caledonia, which we call Scotland, their well-studded boots echoing on the hard surface as they made their 1,000 paces for each mile. (Each pace being a double step, making a Roman mile about 1,600 yards.)

Their progress was marked by milestones. One can still be seen re-erected near the farm of Waterfalls, away from the road. This was to mark the place from which the Earl of Derwentwater and his men started on their ill-fated journey of rebellion in 1715. Another Roman milestone has been re-erected on the roadside to the north of West Woodburn. From a viewpoint here can be seen the route of the Roman road, which leaves the present road towards the fort at Risingham on the Rede.

The Roman road rejoined the present road at Fourlaws Farm. The area traversed is the Vickers range for testing tanks and guns. Challenger tanks have been here on trial. The loops and circles made by their tracks have puzzled aerial pho-

tographers. This is still very much a military area and troops of various European countries can be seen on the way to Otterburn camps as they were in Roman times. Other military reminders are the jet aircraft that screech over at high speed and low altitude in mock attacks on the Otterburn Range.

Also below Fourlaws can be seen the piled debris from the stone quarried for the Ridsdale Ironworks. Abandoned for more than a century the gaunt ruins of the engine house are sometimes mistaken for a castle. Some of the workers' houses

Ridsdale Ironworks on the A68, showing the derelict engine house. Founded in the 1830s, it provided iron for the Newcastle High Level Bridge.

remain in the village and the inn is called "The Gun", a reminder of the military range of Lord Armstrong whose company still survives on Tyneside as Vickers Ltd.

For a century there was railway transport on the Wanney Line from Morpeth to Redesmouth, where it joined the Border Counties Railway from Hexham to Riccarton. Army supplies were carried to West Woodburn and there were troop trains too. There was a regular passenger and goods service as well as special trains on Scenic Excursions, or to Bellingham Fair. Freight could be timber, coal or stone. From West Woodburn eastwards there was a hard climb and locomotives panted under the strain, harsh sounds echoing through the valleys. The pace was so slow at Summit Cottage that it was possible to alight and walk beside the line. From here there was a view across country to the sea. In winter locomotives could be stranded for days in the snow. On the hills can be seen circular stells – walled enclosures which were refuges for the sheep from the icy blasts. The Wanney

Railway closed in 1966, but its track can still be followed on foot, a beautiful scenic route.

There was much industrial activity in former times here – the building of railways being an important part, with numerous coal pits and stone quarries. Field walls were built and trees were planted. There were two woollen mills in the vicin-

Near Quarry House are prehistoric walls and later enclosure walls of stone.

ity. At West Woodburn near the river bridge (1828) there was a "a large woollen cloth manufactory, belonging to Messrs Jeremiah and Silvanus Weir" and at Otterburn "a large woollen manufactory, including a carding and fulling mill and a dyehouse." (Parson) Local wool was used and Otterburn Mill can still be visited today.

Other industries have declined – the ironworks and coalpits have ceased to function as well as a lot of the quarries. There has been considerable activity in the planting of trees, mainly conifers which cover some of the bleaker areas. The farms have returned mainly to pasture and on the moors, the rearing and protection of grouse is promoted. Exploration on foot reveals ancient trackways and old field boundaries. Ruined buildings are frequently found and grass-grown humps indicate buried walls. Research has shown that old field boundaries and features were kept such as old stones as markers. Some walls date back to prehistoric times and have been rebuilt at different periods. Today many have fallen into disuse. Old rigs and furrows show that there has been considerable cultivation of crops, since until the 18th century there was a good deal of subsistence agriculture. People had to grow

4

their own food locally, and "lazy beds" are the old enclosed potato patches.

Old bell pits can be discovered – the earlier type of coalpits, and near Plashetts is a hole that was once a lead mine. In 1828 it was reported "Messrs Milner, Featherstone and Company have been working a lead mine here for some time, but they have not been very successful." (Parson) On the other hand, Thomas Carr owned Tone Hall, "near to which is Tone Colliery and the Tone Pit Inn." Tone Inn is still there, inviting travellers that journey along Dere Street. The Romans would call it a "mansio", from which we get our word "mansion", a place to stay.

There are places to stay for shepherds and others called shielings, which were only used in summertime. Other settlements lasted longer, but there was always change in these remote parts. Population and agriculture rose and declined, depending upon the climate, on plagues and wars. Medieval wars, which were local, meant depopulation. More modern wars, which were far away, meant an increased demand for food supplies and cultivation of the land for corn.

CHAPTER I: FROM FOURLAWS TO KIRKWHELPINGTON

During the 18th century the Agrarian Revolution introduced improvements in crop rotation and in the breeding of cattle and sheep. Northumberland was not backward in these developments, which involved the enclosures of large areas of common land, moorland and waste.

In 1717 Whelpington Common was divided and parts were put under cultivation. The Duke of Somerset (inheritor of Percy lands) acquired some 1900 acres upon which he built four farms – Cowford at the foot of Dawes Moss, Busy Gap west of Catcherside, another at Wolf Crag and the fourth at a place called "Register." Hodgson writing his history in the 1830s said that three of the farms were in ruins and only the fourth, Raechester, remained. It is still there. What happened was that in the 18th century corn and other products were in demand during the French Wars from 1793 to 1815. Prices reached record heights, but after the war in spite of government regulations (Corn Laws) prices declined and marginal land went out of cultivation. But the land was good for sheep and for grouse. Severe game laws were imposed by Tory governments against poachers and enforced by local magistrates. Some landlords established deer parks, and fishing was profitable as well as being a pastime.

Hodgson mentioned the improved turnpike roads as another factor. There were good corn lands over the Border providing cheaper meal and flour, so that this could be exchanged for coal and other products from the English side. In 1663 there were eleven working corn mills in the parishes of Elsdon and Corsenside. When he wrote his history only one was working at Elsdon and very little corn was grown. There was a return to grass for cattle and sheep with increased markets for meat, milk, cheese, butter and wool. He mentions the serious decline of woodland and the necessity of fencing new plantations against the sheep.

"Several large plantations of Scotch firs give a sort of Scandinavian feature to the landscape." (Hodgson)

In 1717 the other landowners sharing the common lands were Sir William Blackett, Gawen Aynsley, Daniel Harle, Sir John Swinburne and the Rector of Whelpington. A result of enclosure could mean the disappearance of villages, now called "deserted medieval villages."

Hodgson described a completely deserted village. "The Village of West Whelpington stood proudly on the northern margin of the Wansbeck, on an elevated plain which slopes gently towards the east and is defended on all sides, especially on the south by a whinstone precipice. It was of oblong form about 440 yards long and consisted of two rows of houses including a large town green, near the centre of which a small circle points out the site of its cockpit, near which has stood a peel house about 23½ by 21½ feet in the inside, having thick walls and a sort of yard or barmkin in front, apparently the only little fortified habitation which

it could ever boast of."

A man named Stote had taken over the land and had "put out 15 farmers", so that "the place is only remarkable for the distinction of its ruins, the beautiful verdure of the site." (Hodgson) It reminded him of Goldsmith's poem, "The Deserted Village".

West Whelpington is near the farm of Cornhills. The next farm westwards is Ferneyrigg, where there is a moated enclosure. In the fields and across the road to the top of Great Wanney were erected a line of boundary stones. On the west side are the initials M M for Mark Milbank. On the east side are the initials W B for Walter (or William) Blackett and T S for Thomas Smith. The date is 1736. The stones are in a straight line and since that date a stone wall has been erected over them which provides direct evidence of the enclosure. The Milbanks of Yorkshire bought lands from the Herons of Chipchase. Hodgson mentioned that Horncastle belonged to Mark Milbank. There was a poor thatched house, which he rebuilt in 1765, on an elevated site above the Wansbeck.

Ray was a medieval village, the ruins of an old tower and fishponds can still be seen near the railway. Hodgson said that the mansion house was in ruins, but later Sir Charles Parsons acquired the estate and built another house there. During World War II the area was used as a wartime timber depot. The woodwork of the hall was affected by rot and it had to be demolished. There was a railway halt on the Wanney Line at Ray. A series of earthworks and encampments can be seen by walking the Wanney Line, but it is private property and permission is needed. It is an area of "game" and when I was there some years ago pheasants were occupying the ruins of the old pele. There are earthworks at Sunnyside near Ray and on either side of the road at Middlerig. A sheepfold stands on the ruins of the old farmhouse.

On the top of Great Wanney there is a prehistoric fortification, which can be reached by footpath. From here are splendid views eastwards to the sea, and the four smoking chimneys of Cambois Power Station mark the mouth of the River Wansbeck. There was once a Great Wanney House below the Crag and Little Wanney House below the crag of that name. From the Great Wanney can be seen the Loughs of Sweethope, the haunt of birds and many fishermen.

I am reminded of Sir Charles Parsons, who spent his leisure time on his Ray estate. One fine morning he went fishing, with a youth rowing him out into the Lough. He was rather hot-tempered and spoke harshly to the rower, who promptly threw his oars into the water and swam ashore, leaving the inventor of "Turbinia" fuming in the middle of the lake. Today it is a popular place for anglers.

At Howick, a deserted village, we see:-
A low plain chapel fronts the morning light
Fast by the silent rivulet. Humbly walk,
O stranger o'er consecrated ground
And on that verdant hillock, which thou seest
Beset with osiers, let they pious hand

7

Sprinkle fresh water from the brook and strew
Sweet smelling flowers. For here doth Edmund rest
The learned shepherd.
(from *Tragedy of a Shepherd* by Mark Akenside)

WEST WHELPINGTON

West Whelpington old village was on an outcrop of the Whin Sill, which makes very good roadstone. The site of the deserted village was excavated over a number of years in advance of quarrying from 1958 to 1976. Then quarrying was discontinued so that much of the settlement still remains. The excavations have been reported in some detail. At the west end were discovered two circular palisaded enclosures, within which were the evidence of several round houses. These were occupied in the Roman and PreRoman periods. Anglo Saxon settlement was likely, but not definitely proven. There was occupation from the 12th to the 18th centuries, though there may have been gaps. The earliest structures were at the west end, which were later abandoned. This may have been the results of raids by the Scots after Bannockburn in 1314.

In 1334 there was a petition for relief from taxation on account of damage by raiding. The rebuilding consisted of four main terraces of longhouses on either side of the green. The houses had crofts to the rear and the pattern shows as a number of small rectangles within larger ones. These are outlined by turf covered walls, which can be seen in the areas that were not quarried.

It is an interesting site to visit, approached by a narrow lane. The Wansbeck flows to the south and around are the characteristic riggs and furrows of what were the open fields, in which some 28 husbandmen had their holdings. There were 28 longhouses and eight cottages, which were reduced in time. Families may well have moved to Cornhills and Horncastle in the 17th century. Final depopulation of West Whelpington came about 1720.

Stott was not directly responsible, as Hodgson was told. The owner was Mark Milbank, a wealthy Newcastle merchant, and the Stotts were tenants at Cornhills, Ferneyrigg and Horncastle. There was yet another new farmstead at Middle Rig. So it seems that separate farmsteads with cottages replaced the old village, which became derelict. The name Cornhills indicates that at this period there was considerable development of arable farming. Of those dispossessed at West Whelpington, some moved to neighbouring farms and others left the area.

The church for the neighbourhood was at Kirkwhelpington, the centre of the parish which overlooks the River Wansbeck and is off the present main road – the old roads ran differently. The road northwards can be seen from the bridge that was built about 1820, below the Rectory. It crosses the fields to West Whitehills and by Knowesgate to Catcherside, where there is now only a farm and a house, which was obviously a bastle. Hodgson wrote "The Scotch street ran through it and it had an ale-house, where the carriers and cadgers in the bell horse times baited and the neighbouring villagers used to meet, so late as the beginning of the last century, to

shoot through long duck guns at the bull's eye for buck's skins. Forty years since there was an old oaken door here, all battered and bored with shot expended in these contentions. But it was not merely with the carousels of the carriers and the thunder of duck guns that Catcherside was famous", (Hodgson) for important people met there. There was also a water mill. Now it is rather interesting as the boundary between the bleaker moorland and the enclosed fields. Belts of trees have been planted to the north, but there is an attractive tree-lined lane from Raechester to Catcherside and Coldwell, coming out on the Cambo road near the disused railway. It makes a most interesting walk. The disused railway is used for walks from Wallington Hall.

CHAPTER II: KIRKWHELPINGTON
AND ITS SURROUNDS

KIRKWHELPINGTON

A general view of **Kirkwhelpington** is obtained from the south, coming up from Little Harle. The village lies to the north of the Wansbeck with the Rectory and Church being the outstanding features. To the east is the Methodist Chapel built in patterned brick, below which on the river is the disused cornmill and the miller's house. A leat fed another mill to the north – the fulling mill, which has been demolished. The village is very attractive. Most of the houses are built of stone and the gardens have splendid displays of flowers in summer. The River Wansbeck is a most alluring feature, flowing beneath the gardens of the old Rectory and Quarry House, burbling beneath a neat arched bridge and moving on to serve the watermills in former times, now providing water for the cattle.

The village formerly had thatched cottages and bastles, but buildings were very much improved by the Duke of Northumberland. One house was a Court House. Hodgson records that 12 cottages were taken down when the new half acre holdings were established. He himself was Vicar here from 1823 until 1832 when he moved to Hartburn. At Kirkwhelpington he wrote much of his *History of Northumberland* and periodically carried out excavations on the Roman Wall and elsewhere. He would set out on Mondays with his horse vehicles carrying men, tools and supplies, returning for his Sunday services. Part of the Vicarage was a little tower, mentioned in 1542. It measured 27 feet by 15 feet internally and the walls were 5 feet in thickness. By Hodgson's time this had been converted into a kitchen. A new house had been built south of it in the 18th century and an attractive garden was developed. This can be seen from the churchyard, and a little plaque beside the door leading to the vicarage records the deaths of two of his children in 1830. In his account of Whelpington he specially mentions a "peel" house, called the Bolt House which "consists of a byer or cowhouse below and the family apartments above viz. an upper room with a boarded floor and a garret both approached by stone stairs on the outside, and the whole covered with thatch. The doorway to the cowhouse is under the landing of the stairs and the door of it is fastened by a strong bolt inside, for which purpose the byer and upper room had a communication by a trap hole, that is, by a horizontal door in a corner of the floor, and a trap or ladder... This was the character of the principal farmhouses in Northumberland a hundred years since." The more substantial houses had vaulted stone basements and freestone slate on the roofs, much safer than thatch.

The Church dedicated to St Bartholomew, is built in a style suitable for a dangerous and windswept countryside. It has a strong square multi-buttressed medieval west tower that could have provided a place of refuge in times of trouble. The west door is not now used and entrance is by a medieval porch on the south side. The medieval doorway is probably not in its original position. Excavations have indicated that the church had aisles. Then these were reduced to transepts,

Kirkwhelpington Church with foursquare west tower. John Hodgson lived at the Rectory.

which in turn were demolished. The result is that the church seems very long. The nave measures 68 feet by 20 feet and the chancel adds a further 34 feet in length. The tower arch contains stone which may have been transferred from a Norman chancel arch. The present chancel and chancel arch are 13th century with the tower added in the 14th century. There was once a west gallery, which has been removed. The font is 17th century but rests on the capital of a medieval pillar. There is a rather ostentatious monument to Gawen Aynsley, who died in 1750 and his wife who died in 1756. The flowery lettering is said to be the work of Thomas Whittell, the Cambo poet and artist. An account written in 1890 states the church "still remains just such a church as the ecclesiastical authorities 100 years ago loved to have. A flat whitewashed ceiling, square high-backed pews, much like cattle pens and of the rudest carpentry of the village, pulpit and sounding board of the same type of art, flat headed cottage windows sashed and glazed with large square panes and a large melancholy gallery at the west end, are the predominant characteristics of this church. The church at Whelpington is one of the very few still left as they were in the days when George III was a young king." (Monthly Chronicle)

Things have improved since then. One of the bells was inscribed "Ave Maria graciae plena", which records the connection of the church with Newminister Abbey, Morpeth. There is a sundial over the door of the porch with the date 1764 and a much eroded inscription – "Hora Pars Vitae – the Hour is part of Life."

The churchyard is full of tombstones recording the village worthies. Within the church is a memorial to Sir Charles Parsons of Ray, who was buried in the church-yard. The old school house and school at the east end of the church have been

closed, but part is used as a Church of England hostel.

John Colling, parish clerk for 63 years at Whelpington, died in 1826. He was a mason who had taken part in the building of Kielder Castle for the Duke, and Rothley and Codger's Castles for the Blacketts of Wallington. Reverend Anthony Hedley was curate at Whelpington from 1814 to 1819. He was a close friend and helper of John Hodgson, who followed him here. He was born in 1777 at Hopefoot near Otterburn. His grandfather, Anthony, had married Mary Brown, a relation of the Browns of Ravenscleugh; so that he was related to the famous Lancelot Brown, known as Capability Brown who was born at Kirkharle.

Hedley was educated at Glasgow and Edinburgh Universities, after which he was appointed tutor by the Marquess of Bath of Longleat. He became directly acquainted with Capability Brown's landscaping and himself became an enthusiast gardener, improving wherever he went. He returned north as curate of St John Lee, near Hexham and was later appointed to Whitfield. He purchased the Roman site of Vindolanda or Chesterholm, where he built himself a house in Abbotsford style. He was a keen antiquarian and excavated at Housesteads with Hodgson. He also excavated at his own Vindolanda where, going out on a bitter January morning, he caught a fatal chill in 1835. Hodgson in his History of Northumberland, acknowledged a great debt to him.

KIRKHARLE – BIRTH PLACE OF CAPABILITY BROWN

The name of Lancelot Brown reminds us that we should now travel three miles south through wooded countryside, which he helped to develop, to his birth place at Kirkharle. The present village lies to the south of the River Wansbeck on the Kirkharle Burn, a tributary. Originally it was to the south-west of the church and the hall. When Lancelot was born in 1716, some improvements were being made in agriculture by local landowners such as the Blacketts, Loraines and Swinburnes. The lands to the south of the wild moorland wastes lent themselves to enclosure and the planting of trees. A view was presented of transfer from wilderness to meadows and parkland. Lancelot Brown grew up under this influence and himself took part in the process. According to the Parish Records he was baptised on 30 August 1716 in the church of St Wilfrid, Kirkharle. A memorial plaque was set up to him in 1983, 200 years after his death. He was the fifth child of William Brown of Kirkharle, related to the Browns of Ravenscleugh near Elsdon. William Brown probably worked on the Loraine's estate at Kirkharle. His elder son became steward, marrying Jane Loraine, Sir William Loraine's younger daughter.

Lancelot was educated until the age of 16 – quite a long time for a boy to stay at school in those days. First of all he was taught at Kirkharle and the neighbouring village of Cambo, the estate village of Wallington Hall, which was the Blacketts' house.

Dorothy Stroud comments "There can be little doubt that young Lancelot, wending his way homeward when lessons were over, paused to watch the labourers at their various jobs and noticed the silvery Wansbeck take on a new loveliness as

its surroundings gradually changed from untidy wastes to orderly fertility." (Stroud) He must have made up his mind to take part. Though he did not work on the Wallington Estate, he was to provide plans for Sir Walter Blackett later when he was an accepted national figure.

After leaving school in 1732 he went into the service of Sir William Loraine at Kirkharle. He had probably been working as a gardener's boy in his spare time before this. All country boys would be gainfully employed in garden or in field. Lancelot had an apprenticeship of seven years during which time he rapidly became the chief assistant to his employer. He would get to know his job from the earth itself, and he gained a feeling for plants and trees, knowing where to put them and how to develop them. The vegetable garden was valued by him, but it was put in its proper place away from the house at some distance and sheltered by a wall. It had a commercial but not a scenic value.

Sir William inherited his estate in 1718. He restored the Church providing it with strong walls and a stone floor. He built "a new mansion house (of his own plan and contrivance) with all offices, out houses, gardens, fountains, fishponds (the first regular ones ever made in that county) belonging to them " (Hodgson)

A contemporary account speaks of him as expert in architecture, planting trees and making enclosures. He planted above 24,000 trees and 488,000 quicksets for enclosures. In the gardens he planted 580 fruit trees Lancelot would see all of this and helped in much of it. He became so accomplished that he was borrowed for a time by Mr Shaftoe of Benwell Towers, Newcastle. It might be explained here how he got his nickname "Capability." The term does not apply to himself, his ability was obvious. When he went about to advise on the development of landscapes, he would assess what he called its "capabilities." We would speak of possibilities of improvement.

He decided in 1739 to move south seeking his fortune as many others did. It must have been a wrench to leave his family and move 200 miles to Wotton in Oxfordshire where he took a job. From here in 1740 he went to Lord Cobham's set at Stowe, which had become the most celebrated place in the country for its gardens. The gardens received many distinguished visitors. They were the work of Charles Bridgeman who was followed by William Kent. Brown became head gardener and so met many of Lord Cobham's friends and relations. Kent was an architect responsible for buildings, and to a distinguished foreign visitor who later enquired, "Who laid out these grounds"? the reply was, "Originally a Mr Brown, who went by the name of Capability".

In 1750 after Lord Cobham's death he moved to Hammersmith and set up his own practice as a landscapist. He became friendly with Henry Holland, architect and builder, and they worked together. Brown extended his range of commissions to the whole country, but did not serve abroad. A list of his works would fill a book.

In 1759 he was appointed Royal Gardener to Kings George II and then George III with a residence at Hampton Court. William Pitt, Prime Minister wrote of him –

"he shares the private hours of the King, dines familiarly with his neighbour of Syon (the Duke of Northumberland) and sits at the tables of all the House of Lords ... he is deserving of the great regard shown to him, for I know him upon a long acquaintance to be an honest man and of sentiments much above his birth."

Brown did a lot of work for this William Pitt, Earl of Chatham. Brown disliked the formal garden and was accused of destroying many. Nor did he approve of long avenues of trees and straight roads within the area of a country mansion. His attitude to landscape was practical – gentle slopes and contours with lavish sweeps of trees. He created what might be called the park-land. There were clumps of trees, individual trees and shelter belts, but all seemed natural and not planted. He would hate the regimented forests that we see about us.

Horace Walpole wrote of him – "Such was the effect of his genius that he will be least remembered. So closely did he copy nature that his works will be mistaken for it." He organised the landscape into great natural curves, crowned them with clumps of trees, natural forest and boundary screens. The ha-ha or sunken wall with ditch was used to protect lawns and garden areas from cattle and sheep. Barriers were provided, but views from the house were not obstructed.

Water was a most interesting object in the landscape and Brown dammed small streams to provide extensive lakes or a series of pools. The house could be reflected in the water, which was permanent but not stagnant. There were ornamental bridges and buildings in a natural landscape. In Northumberland the best examples

Kirkharle Church, in the village where Capability Brown was born. It has a medieval font from Newcastle All Saints

14

of his work are at Alnwick Castle and Hulne Park, where the landscape was transformed.

Another example is shown by Rothley Lakes on the Alnwick Road, one on either side. The Ewesley Burn was dammed to provide the supply of water. He was also responsible for landscape work at Hesleyside and Wallington. The man was forgotten, but his work remained. It was not until 1950 that the first full scale biography of him appeared which was written by Dorothy Stroud. Since then his achievements have become much better known, and his native county can be proud of him.

The church at Kirkharle is approached by a field road, past the site of the old village with the hall eastwards. This was reduced in size during the last century after being purchased by Major Anderson of Little Harle. One wing remains with the farm buildings. The church overlooks the burn and the wide curving medieval plough rigs in the field. There are many grave slabs in the floor of the church to the Loraine family. The medieval font is specially interesting. It once served in the Newcastle Church of All Hallows, which was knocked down about 1786 when the new All Saints Church was constructed. The font was transferred to Kirkharle. It carries the coats of arms of several important families including the Loraines. On the way to the church is a grim reminder of earlier times – a monument to Robert Loraine who was killed on his way from church (1483) by some Scots "in revenge for his good services to his country against their thefts and robbery." (Hodgson)

LITTLE HARLE

"Little Harle Tower, a fine grey coloured mass of towers and parapeted walls, has a front of 130 feet, and is bosomed on all sides but the south in a deep grove of forest trees. The tower to the west is the most ancient, and in the survey of 1542 is described as "in good reparations" and "of the inheritance of Thomas Fenwyke."

The entrance is by a spacious hall on the east built in 1809 by Lady Charles Aynsley after a plan by Atkinson suited to the castellated style of the rest of the building and emblazoned on the front with the arms of Aynsley and numerous quarterings of the Athol family." (Hodgson)

The 18th century improvements included some very fine plasterwork done by Italian craftsmen, who worked at neighbouring Wallington.

In 1833 Thomas Anderson of Newcastle purchased both Kirkharle and Little Harle. The Andersons had owned Anderson Place in Newcastle, a fine house where Charles I stayed. A chimney piece was transferred to Little Harle and a number of paintings including Carmichael's "Barge Day on the River Tyne". About 1865 Thomas Anderson built a battlemented tower to Little Harle and added another wing eastwards. These Victorian towers were status symbols, hard to maintain in modern times, and that at Eshott and Little Harle have been demolished. This makes Little Harle difficult to see in the trees from the Wallington direction.

15

NEW DEANHAM HALL

The road from Kirkharle follows the Rothbury road to the junction with the Otterburn road and crosses towards Wallington. On the left of the road is the attractive farmhouse of Shielhill, which takes guests and where furniture is made. On the other side of the road across the fields is New Deanham Hall, a very good example of what a 17th century house was like. The articles for building were that

New Deanham Hall, between Capheaton and Wallington. Built in 1670, it is little altered 300 years later.

William Nicholson, 28 October 1689, agreed to build for John Fenwick of Deanham, gentleman, "one good new house, in length three lowe rooms each six yards square within the walls, besides the partitions, and ten foot high: and to dig and make one cellar under the hall or middle room, to be six yards square and six foot and six inches high under the dormants – and to build three chambers or upper rooms over the said three lower rooms, of the same proportion and height of the three of the three lower rooms, with four garrets over the said chambers and four pinion gavells in the garrets and build the walls of the garrets one yard above the upper floor: and place 12 windows on the front and one window at each gavell end the windows all of hewn stone. All the walls to be sufficiently built with stone and lime, with hewn stone coynes and so many chimneys of hewn stone as shall be necessary: and also to build a convenient staircase without the house of stone steps, four foot long upon the steps within the walls of the said staircase. The house to be well slated, plastered, glassoned, flowered, doored, locked and keyed and the kitchens and cellar flagged and that the said William Nicholson find all stone,

16

lyme, timber, workmanship and other materials – on consideration that John Fenwick pay him £260: lead all the hewn stone from the quarry at Bolam and 20 fother of timber felled within 12 miles of Deanham; and provide a great hammer and a gavelock to be restored when the work is done: and find grass and hay and four bowles of oats for the said William Nicholson during the whole time he shall be employed in the said work." (Hodgson)

In the construction of roads and houses transport was the most expensive item. The house of 1669 still stands, a modest building situated between the more expensive mansions of Capheaton and Wallington.

CAPHEATON

Capheaton, south of Old Deanham and Wallington, is reached by turning off the Pontcland road. It is still hidden in trees, but the approach is now more open,

Capheaton Hall was designed and built by Robert Trollope for Sir John Swinburne in 1668. Pevsner describes its style as 'provincial and enduring Baroque'.

since a great avenue of beech trees was felled in 1982. They had stood for some 200 years, part of the landscaping by the Swinburnes, but not in Capability's style. It was called the Silver Lonnen, since workmen there had found a hoard of silver, which included Roman and Saxon work. Much of it was broken and dispersed, but some was saved.

The Swinburnes have long been at Capheaton, but in the 17th century the link was almost severed. In 1642 John Swinburne was murdered at Meldon Gate by

John Salkeld. The murderer escaped justice on account of the Civil War. The Swinburnes were Catholic and John's son was sent abroad for education and was conveniently forgotten. However, one of the Radcliffe family visited a monastery and recognised the features of young Swinburne. Enquiries showed that he was the heir to the estates and so he returned to England. He was knighted by King Charles II and married Catherine Lawson, whose mother was a Fenwick of Meldon. Sir John and his wife lived at Meldon, where his father was murdered, while Capheaton Hall was built, replacing the old castle. The architect was Robert Trollop of Newcastle, who designed "a goodly house after the modern fashion with Courts, garden and bowling green." There was to be built "one new house at Capheaton, near unto the ground or place where one old building or castle is now standing, which shall be in length eight and twenty yards and in breadth 20 yards with a cellar underneath the whole front. The first floor is to be two feet above ground and the second floor 13 feet higher.

"That there be on every of the three said floors six rooms besides closets and passages and a chimney in each room. The front to be of hewn stone or ashlar work with rustic pilasters from the ground table to the mudyllyons and to have a balcony built over the hall door 10 foot square supported by two pillars and two half pillars with a stone tarrest on each side below and flagged at the bottom and have a tarrest of wood ballisters above and leaded on the top – both ends to be built of hewn stone or ashler worke with rustic pilasters above." (Hodgson)

A ten feet projection at the back was for the enlarging of the stairs and the chimneys were of stone. Particulars were given about the roofing and the windows. The lower windows were to have iron bars. The outside was to be finished by 11 November 1669, and Trollop was to be paid £500. He was to have use of all stone, timber, lead, iron and glass from the old castle. Any extra stone, timber, lime and sand could be obtained from the estate locally, though Sir John also owned Edlingham Castle.

Hodgson adds that at Capheaton Hall – "There is a large bird's eye view of this building still preserved there as it was left by Trollop, with the family of the builder issuing from the gates to meet a party of their neighbours, the Lorains of Kirkharle, come on a visit and the family coach is introduced in full equipage to give effect to the courteous ceremony."

The painting was by Robert Crosby and dates to 1674. It seems rather surprising that such a house existed in Northumberland at this date. Many people think that there would still be military structures. A century after the picture Capheaton was altered. The architect, William Newton, constructed a new north front in correct classical style. This became the main entrance and the carriage approach through the avenue of beech trees came from the north. Fortunately the front shown on the picture is still there and there is no road approach to it. A ha-ha separates the hall and its gardens from the fields. The trees and the lake westwards would win the approval of Capability Brown. "A little to the south west of the village and in sight of it, is the lake, hemmed on the south and east by a deep wood,

studded with woody islets and gay with boats that all the summer long skim its surface with a playfulness and skill, as if the hull and cordage and sails of each were the body of a living animal that delighted to "take its pastimes" on the waters. A quarter of a mile away at Sandybreas, a lead mine was worked to some advantage prior to 1786, but abandoned on account of a steam engine becoming necessary to draw water and from an apprehension that extending the workings under such a power, might drain the springs which supply the lake." (Hodgson)

Capheaton Castle is said to have been a substantial moated structure, which suffered in the Civil War. The outside chapel is a ruin, but there was a chapel within the new house, and there were two hiding holes for Catholic priests or other refugees. The Earl of Derwentwater (1715), when faced with defeat at Preston, sent his huntsman to take his papers from Dilston to Capheaton. They were carried away safely and hidden till the time of the 1745 rebellion. A mason, called in to repair the roof, had seen the hidden boxes with coats of arms on them. He informed Sir William Middleton of Belsay, who searched with a party. He secured the Derwentwater records which were sent to London and disappeared. Fortunately the excellent Swinburne records are deposited in the County Record Office, a quarry for researchers.

In the last century, Sir John Swinburne lived to the age of 99, a remarkable character. He was very fond of a grandson named Algernon Charles Swinburne, who became a famous poet. We are given a picture of this wild young man, who often stayed at Capheaton, riding down the avenue at break-neck speed with his red hair flying on his way to Wallington to visit Lady Pauline Trevelyan and her artistic friends. Sir John Swinburne, who built the Hall, died in 1706, and was buried in Kirkwhelpington church.

CHAPTER III: WALLINGTON

The way down from Capheaton to Wallington provides a fascinating spectacle. Westwards can be seen the woods of Little Harle and Wallington. In the middle view appear New Deanham, and northwards Cambo with the eye-catching Rothley Castle, a folly and landmark in the distance. Beyond are increasing hills rising to the Simonsides. Eastwards Shaftoe Crags and Harnham Hall come into view and extensive fields of grassland with hedgerows. The stone walls are characteristic of the rougher landscapes. The narrow road towards Wallington passes New Deanham as described, and reaches the Corn Road near Old Deanham, which confusingly is much later in date, though it has prehistoric standing stones in the field. The road turns at right angles and runs parallel to the Wansbeck, again with delightful views of Wallington.

It reaches a remarkably designed rainbow arched bridge of c.1750 over the Wansbeck, built by Sir Walter Blackett at his own cost – £500.

Wallington Bridge, built over the Wansbeck in 1760 by James Payne for Sir William Blackett.

The plans for the Corn Road had included only a ford, but this bridge, to Sir Walter and many others since, has been both an asset and a thing of beauty.

Wallington is recorded in 1541 as "a strong tower and a stone house" belonging to Sir John Fenwick. Sir John had other towers at Rothley, Hartington and across the fields at the farm of Fawns. Thomas Fenwick had the tower of Little Harle –

the Fenwicks were a powerful family.

In 1689 Sir John Fenwick mortgaged Wallington to William Blackett. Fenwick had married a daughter of the Earl of Carlisle and was a very talented man. He continued to support the Stuarts after the expulsion of James II in 1689 and was accused of treason against King William III. He was condemned to death, but had his revenge indirectly. His horse, Sorel, was acquired by the King, and in 1702 it caught a hoof in a mole hill at Hampton Court. The King was heavily thrown and died from his injuries. William I and II also fell from their horses and died.

The Blacketts were wealthy merchants of Newcastle with interests in coal and lead. Their house, formerly the Greyfriars, was later called Anderson Place, an estate within Newcastle itself. Sir William, as he became, was MP and Mayor of Newcastle several times. He continued to buy property and Wallington was his country retreat. He pulled down the Fenwick building, the vaults of which became the cellars of the new house. His son, also Sir William, gained his wealth, but not his ability.

He managed to escape being involved in the 1715 rebellion, but won the favour of neither side. When he married in 1723 there were great celebrations at Wallington and the Devil's Punch Bowl, a hollow in the rock, on Shaftoe Crags, flowed with free drink. He had no legitimate children, but a daughter by his mistress Elizabeth Ord. In his will he left his property to his daughter Elizabeth on condition that she should wed his nephew Walter Calverley. Walter obligingly married the lady and took the property, emerging as Sir Walter Calverley Blackett. He immediately took action to improve the Wallington estate and other properties with their mines and mills.

Sir William Blackett had erected the present Hall described as "a great stone block standing square to the points of the compass, its four faces each about 120 feet in length. Most of Sir William's time was spent in his magnificent residence in Newcastle and Wallington house was regarded primarily as a shooting box. It contained little or no adornment, while the interior was entirely lacking in the expected refinements. There were no corridors and no principal staircase, the upper rooms which led out of each other, being approached by a few miserable sets of stairs in each corner of the house. Outside the surrounding lands consisted of ragged, unfenced crofts and pastures, undrained fells and moorland. The estate map drawn up in 1728 exists and Sir George Trevelyan has described how it shows "no enclosures except rude earth banks which could be climbed by the cattle: no roads other than horse or cart tracks winding from farm to farm across the fields and nothing in the way of timber on the whole vast area save a few self sown trees sheltering in the slopes of some of the northern ravines." (Stroud)

Hodgson describes the setting of Wallington.

"The character of the scenery about the house is breadth and variety. From this terrace in the south front, the rich lawn of the Park, interspersed with fine old trees, slopes boldly off to the Wansbeck, the opposite side of which is shaded with hang-

ing woods, over which the prospect ends in the dark and rugged brown of Shaftoe Crags. On the road about halfway from the bridge to the house, the view through the park into the woody and undulating grounds of Little Harle is rich and diversified: but the broadest and finest view of the place is from different points of the knoll in the Deanham grounds over which the Alemouth Road passes eastwards from Shillaw Hill (Shielhill). Here the landscape is composed in front of the winding and woody banks of the Wansbeck, then broad vistas of the lawn in the park, backed with woods of vast extend and venerable growth, beyond which rises the castle crowned head of Rothley Crags and further on, air tinted heights and purple moors mellowing and melting into the blue summit of Simonside."

This gives some idea of the changes that took place under the Blacketts and later the Trevelyans. Nowadays things have to change because the trees are so old and in due course have to be replaced. Trees have been planted by the Northumberland and Newcastle Society as a tribute to Lady Mary Trevelyan. Her husband, Sir Charles Trevelyan, gave Wallington to the National Trust in 1941, and it is one of their most important properties, attracting many visitors. On both sides of the road are gardens, plantations of trees and ornamental lakes, fed by a small stream which eventually finishes in the River Wansbeck. Quite remarkable is the beautiful scenery it traverses.

Wallington Hall today appears attractively through the trees as viewed from the road. In the foreground are a number of dragons' or griffins' heads. They were

Griffins at Wallington Hall, which had formerly adorned Bishopsgate, London and Rothley Park belonging to the Blacketts.

brought from London in ballast for Sir Walter Calverley Blackett. In his time coal was being mined at Cambo and coal from his other mines was shipped to London. These figures and others were obtained when Bishopsgate, London, was being demolished.

In Sir Walter's time they were set up as figures in Rothley Deer Park to the north of Cambo. Rothley or Roadley Castle was a part of it and included massive rocky crags. The castle, a folly, very carefully sited, was an eyecatcher from many directions. On account of vandalism the figures were later brought down to Wallington.

In the Hall itself, the interior was artistically decorated by Italian craftsmen, and the Blacketts collected pictures, porcelain and all kinds of curios. As time passed, the property was inherited by the Trevelyans, a Cornish family. Sir John Trevelyan succeeded his Blackett uncle in 1777, but he preferred the south and his son John came to live at Wallington.

Sir Walter Blackett had also constructed the Clock House, which closed the courtyard to the north of the Hall. It is a delightful building, designed by Payne who also designed the bridge. Above the central arched opening is the cupola with the clock, still one fingered. On either side are coach house and stables, with cottages for estate workers. Cambo is the estate village at a convenient distance to the north. Again it has attractive stone built houses and gardens. The old tower called a "peel house" is now used as a shop, but its strength is manifest. The old chapel

Cambo Tower, built in medieval times for defence and now used as a post office.

decayed, but in 1842 the new church of Holy Trinity was built. The tall west tower was added in 1883, becoming a landmark. Of special interest inside are some curious medieval grave slabs in a very good state of preservation.

In the centre of the village is a fountain in the form of a dolphin to supply fresh water. It is inscribed with the Latin words "Futuri Haud Immemor Oevi" – "not forgetting future generations".

Sir Walter Trevelyan was a teetotaller and closed the inn called "The Two Queens". The old school is used as the Village Hall, and a stone tablet reminds us that Capability Brown was educated here. Trevelyan was a remarkable man, a scholar and specially interested in science, natural history and archaeology. There is a museum with many fine specimens in Wallington Hall. He was very much concerned with health and the good

of society. His wife was an accomplished artist, and many distinguished painters and writers visited Wallington. Lord Macaulay, a relative and famous historian stayed and wrote at Wallington. According to visitors the house was none too comfortable since it was constructed as a quadrangle about an open courtyard. It was noisy and it was draughty. Ruskin, a frequent visitor, suggested that it should be roofed over. John Dobson was responsible for the construction of the central Hall. Pauline Trevelyan was the inspiring genius for its decoration so that it almost became an epitome of the history of Northumberland. William Bell Scott (1811-1880), Director of the School of Design, Newcastle, provided eight large canvases showing historical scenes. They had authentic background and living people were used as models including Trevelyans, visitors and local workers. The main scenes were the building of Hadrian's Wall; Grace Darling; Coal and Iron on Tyneside; the Death of Bede; the Charlton Spur; Bernard Gilpin at Rothbury; Cuthbert on Lindisfarne and the Danes attacking the Tyne. A series of roundels portray famous Northumbrians from Hadrian to George Stephenson. In the upper spandrels between arches are illustrations of the ballad of Chevy Chase. On the lower pillars are flowers painted by Pauline and, it is said, John Ruskin. All this greatly added to the attractions and comfort of the house, which now visitors can enjoy.

Outside there are many walks for visitors through the gardens and woodlands and along the Wansbeck. Lady Mary Trevelyan was responsible for the walled garden. A number of lead figures look down from the 18th century mellow brick wall. From the gazebo adorned by a Trevelyan owl are widespread views over the meadows and woodland, the Wansbeck Bridge and Shaftoe Crags.

Hutchinson (1778) gives another view.

"On our gaining the summit of the eminence, the country opened upon us beautifully: we now looked down upon the rich vale where Wallington stands, extending towards the south east to a great distance, terminated by a view of the sea. The country before we gained this situation was for some miles unpleasant, little planted and ill cultivated: but this prospect recompensed all the fatigue the eye had endured in the sameness of the preceding passage."

Approaching Cambo "The prospect here is extensive and noble: some coalworks to the right before the nearer ground, but all beyond is a happy composition." (Hutchinson) Today it is hard to believe how extensive the coal pits were hereabouts in the 18th century. They were often bell pits sunk in a line along the coal seam. They scarred the landscape, but often landowners as at Wallington planted them over with trees so that they were hidden and forgotten. There was considerable mining about Deanham and Shaftoe and though the coal was used for local fires, furnaces and kilns, some was sent down the Tyne. Carts taking coal to the ships could bring the stone or tile ballast back to Wallington.

Hutchinson in passing mentions another development of that time – enclosures, which led to unemployment of labourers and rural depopulation. In this neighbourhood a number of villages went out of existence, replaced by separate farms and cottages. "A few great farm houses and hamlets appear rarely scattered over vast

tracts of land." (Hutchinson)

Proceeding northwards, he went out of his way to see Rothley Castle, built as a folly by Sir Walter Blackett.

"Our fatigue was but ill recompensed, for we found this object of our anxious curiosity, no other than an ornamental structure composed of a square tower, flanked with a curvated wall, embattled and pierced with loop holes and each wing terminated with a bastion: the situation romantic, on the banks of a broken precipice.." (Hutchinson) He also describes the "awkward images of a goat and a staring stag". There were broken sculptures, griffins, cornices, the lamb and flag of Calverley and worst of all the jawbones, ribs and member of a whale. But from this place the lord could view his landscape far and wide.

WAYS TO WALLINGTON – KNOWESGATE

When the new road was constructed north of Kirkwhelpington a place on the map called Know became Knowesgate and here when the Wanney Line was constructed a station was erected. When it was in use, coal wagons, cattle wagons and timber wagons could be seen. The railway now provides an interesting walk, while the most prominent feature on the landscape is a wind vane to provide electric power. The huge limestone quarries are now being filled. Stone for limeburning was carried on a waggonway to the kilns at Rugeley, situated on the railway. The four-arched Hartington kilns can be seen on the hillside to the north – these are preserved.

Aerial view of Fawns, a former Fenwick stronghold near Wallington. Earthworks, ditches, fishponds and building foundations can be seen. (© University of Newcastle upon Tyne)

Another feature was Mary's Castle, now woodland. Here was St Mary's Close and Gawen Aynsley pulled down the old farmhouse, and built "a new house and offices with squareheaded and emblazoned gables". (Hodgson) It was called "Mary's Castle" and no doubt was intended to rival Rothley Castle. On the other side of the road a lane leads to a farm called Fawns. In 1542 Sir John Fenwick had a "lytle pele house or Bastell" at a place called "Sawnes". I wonder if the name was changed later – Armstrong has "Fauns" and the neighbouring farm was called Elf Hills.

Fawns consists of a mound that once carried a stone tower. It is surrounded by a deep ditch and overlooks a large enclosure which has a strong bank and deep ditch. This also was walled and within are the foundations of a number of buildings. The moats or ditches took water and there are several fish ponds. In the adjacent fields are the old ridge and furrow systems. It is now usual to find a moated site like this and so it deserves special mention. There is footpath across the fields to Broomhouse and Wallington.

SOUTH MIDDLETON

Another way from Kirkwhelpington follows the Wansbeck along a gated road to Walkmill House. The leat to carry the water can still be seen, but the mill itself has gone; it was a fulling mill important in the making of cloth. The other mill was the corn mill. There is a ford to Dean House Farm and from the rising road the

South Middleton Deserted Village, one of the finest in the country, showing the old house and garden sites with medieval plough riggs. (© University of Newcastle upon Tyne).

Wansbeck can be viewed. Littleharle is just visible in the trees. The land is divided by old stone walls – walls of several periods and re-used stones, some being river boulders. There are a number of earthworks and near the gate at the other end of the field are the remains of a farm house called Hare Willows, which was pulled down about 1820.

The road continues to Wallington, whence we follow the Wansbeck eastwards. The water troughs for the horses on the Newcastle turnpike can be seen and the old milestone near Garden House. On the other side of the river is Scarlet Hall Farm, in the fields of which are the remains of a deserted village.

In the fields of Wallington Newhouses is a moated site, medieval, but which may date back to Roman times. There are many signs of prehistoric man about, standing stones and banked enclosures. At Middleton Bridge on the Bolam Road can be seen the deserted village of South Middleton, which W G Hoskins considered to be one of the best ten in the entire country. It is a protected archaeological site and cannot be ploughed. Best examined on an aerial photograph, it appears very well in winter snow or when the sun's rays are low, lighting the humps and darkening the hollows. The village street can be seen with double rectangular enclosures on each side. They are called tofts (house sites) and crofts (enclosed small fields). There can also be seen the old plough riggs and furrows coming up to the enclosures.

Middleton Mill Farm is to the east and the mill, which probably served the villagers, still stands. The village was depopulated in the middle of the 18th century.

The neighbouring farm of Corridge has a house which dates back to the 17th century and some of the buildings are older, probably part of a larger settlement. There is a building used as a barn, which may have been a chapel. Another unusual building is a dovecote with a privy beneath. The road continues to Bolam West House, a point from which various explorations can be made, most effectively on foot.

SHAFTOE

From Bolam West House there is a lane westwards – a farm way and footpath. At the first gate overlooked by beech trees is a large mound and a tall standing stone called the Poind and His Man. On the map it is designated as a tumulus or prehistoric burial mound. It was excavated in 1718 when a stone coffin was found, but no human remains, only some burnt material. The other stone standing at this time was transferred to Wallington and stands beside a lake. Hodgson states that there was another barrow or pinfold which was demolished to make field walls. The Roman Road called Devil's Causeway passes the tumulus, being about 24 feet wide. In a treeless landscape the mound could be a suitable spot for making the alignment of the road by the Romans. In 1552 "the watch be kept at the two stones, the Poind and His Man, with 2 men nightly",(Hodgson) from Bolam. This was to give warning of any Scottish reivers. The pathway across the field merges with the Salters Road from the coast to Scotland (salt was obtained from sea salt pans,

which was liable like whisky to a heavy duty). In Elsdon churchyard on this route is the tombstone of Thomas Wilson who died in 1778 "officer for the duty of salt".

Our path leads to a rocky precipice through which is a gap called Salter's Nick. From the height of the rocks a wide area of landscape can be viewed, distinguishing the meadow, the woodland, the rocky areas of poor pasture. On top of the rocks of Shaftoe Crags are the earthworks of an ancient enclosure and beneath overhanging rocks are shelters that were inhabited in prehistoric times. These can be investigated from the lower ground, and further south is another rocky ridge on which is perched what has been called the Devil's Punch Bowl. The area is also the site of a prehistoric multivallate hill fort, of which the ramparts and internal divisions can be clearly seen. The Punch Bowl is so called because eroded into the upper surface of the rock are circular cavities. At times they were filled with drink, for instance to celebrate the marriage of Sir William Blackett in 1775. Another rock is called the Piper's Chair and beneath is a deep cave called Shaftoe Hall, which was used for both human habitation and hiding – men as well as foxes.

Further eastwards was the now deserted village of East Shaftoe. Some of the house sites can still be seen as ruined walls and the old road is still used. At the east end of the village was a chapel with a burial ground. Some of the stones and monuments have been transferred to East Shaftoe Hall, an important building.

The oldest part is a tower house to the west with very strong walls and a rib vaulted basement. There are the remains of the early stair turret. Additions have been made to the house at different periods, and it is a Grade 1 Listed building. The old font stands before the house, and built into the garden wall of one of the buildings is an impressive medieval grave cover, decorated with cross, shears, a sword and coat of arms, possibly those of the Aynsley family. The chapel was excavated in 1831 by Lord Decies of Bolam Hall and to Bolam we pay our next visit.

BOLAM

The road eastwards from Bolam West Houses passes two ancient hill forts. To the south is the remarkable Slate Hill, which was much quarried for roofing stone. The interior of the fort was destroyed, but the ramparts remain and are most impressive. They can be reached from Bolam Country Park and from the present field wall a most amazing picture of the countryside can be obtained.

Huckhoe Hill, the fort on the other side of the road is partly quarried and partly overgrown with trees. It was excavated some years ago and was occupied for several hundred years in pre-Roman times. The first defences were timber palisades set in the stone of the site. Later they were replaced by stone walls and the foundations of circular hut walls can be picked out. From this place too there are views over the Wansbeck Valley and the line of the old railway. The Devil's Causeway passes to the west, continuing to Highlaws and after crossing the Wansbeck to Marlish and Hartburn.

The line of the old Salters Road can be seen, as well as the old field systems.

The road reaches the wooded parkland to the west of Bolam. In the trees on a rocky mound are the earthworks of Bolam Castle, once the head of a barony. Hodgson saw a double rampart and ditches, but since that time trees have grown over it. Bolam Hall, a Georgian mansion, was the headquarters of Lord Decies. Hodgson adds details about the improvement of the landscape – "the beauty that the hills and grounds of Bolam are every year acquiring, are chiefly the work of the present proprietor, who to give employment to the poor, in the scarce and disastrous winters of 1816 and 1817, converted the splashy lands of Bolam bog into a fair expanse of water, and has covered the rough and ferny hillsides to the north of it with plantations, that have since been extended into other parts of the estate". (Hodgson)

Today the lake and the surrounding woodlands are a Country Park. Hodgson wrote "The old town of Bolam, which has its grant of a market and fair from Edward I in 1305, consisted of a castle at its head, the church and manse of the rectory, and two rows of houses running east and west beyond them, enclosing a town green and traditionally said to have once consisted of 200 slated houses, consequently of a population of about 900 persons, whose employment is said to have been chiefly in harness and saddlemaking". During the time of the Scottish Wars this was particularly important and no doubt much smithy work and the forging or iron took place. The Devil's Causeway was until the 18th century one of the main roads to Scotland, leading from Corbridge to Berwick. The village has disappeared, but evidence of it can be seen in the pasture land between Bolam Hall and the church. It probably extended beyond the church.

When Bolam Hall was built excavations revealed stonework that had suffered from fire. In 1584 there is a report that the village had been raided and burnt. No doubt there were other occasions. Hodgson wrote that the houses had disappeared by 1810, which no doubt was the policy of the landed proprietor, who did not wish to view a number of tumbledown cottages. Servants could live in the lodges, outhouses and stables.

The church dedicated to St Andrew is one of the finest in the county. It has a tall unbuttressed west tower, which is late Saxon in date, having narrow windows. Entrance is by a porch at the south door and the earliest features within are of the Norman period – altered tower arch and windows and the round chancel arch. The chancel had an apse at the east end, but was later extended. There were both north and south aisles. The north aisle has disappeared, whereas the south aisle had been widened and the Reymes Chapel added. Here is the legless effigy of Robert de Reymes of Shortflatt and Aydon Castle who died in 1342. There are a number of grave covers, carrying floriated crosses, in the chapel and other monuments in the chancel. During World War II a bomb crashed into the church through a window, but fortunately did not explode.

From the church are views over the Wansbeck Valley and in particular Angerton Steads, Angerton Station and Angerton Hall. The narrow road winds on to Hartburn village and we now have to look at the course of the Hart Burn, tributary of the Wansbeck.

CHAPTER IV: THE HARTBURN, TRIBUTARY OF THE WANSBECK

The Hart Burn is made up of a number of streams that emerge from Harwood, Ottercops and Kirkwhelpington Common. The Ottercops and Fairnley burns meet at the bastle house of Fairnley. It measures 42½ ft by 23 ft with 3½ ft walls. It housed the cattle on the ground floor and living quarters were above. In 1713 it was altered by the Blacketts and until recently it was used as farm buildings. It has been restored as a residence, approached from the Corn Road. Opposite are the four arched lime kilns of High Hartington and below stands Hartington Hall on the Hart Burn itself. Hereabouts Hodgson found a causeway of flat slab stones, used to cover marshy ground and providing a solid way for pack animals and pedestrians.

HARTINGTON

At Hartington in 1541 there was "a strong bastelle" belonging to Sir John Fenwick and kept in good repair. It has been modified with a higher roof and new windows to make a modern residence. The walls are thick and the farm buildings have been converted into housing and a garden centre, which takes the old name of Herterton. At one time the village was much larger, and there was a chapel at Kirkhill nearby. Some medieval grave slabs have been built into a wall. A farm further north has the name of Gallowshill, where presumably was a medieval gallows. There is on the Wallington estate at Harwood Head, Winter's Gibbet, monument to a murder of 1792.

The stream that passes eastwards is called the Delf Burn and the only pottery on it was a field kiln, making tiles for drainage. The farm of Donkin Rigg was an old assembly place for cattle which were being driven to Newcastle. The Rothbury railway took over, and at its junction with the Wanney Railway at Scots Gap is the present day sheep and cattle mart. In the last century Sir Walter Trevelyan would only allow a Temperance Hotel to be built. This has become the headquarters of the National Trust in Northumberland. The Rothbury railway was much used by William Armstrong in his development of Cragside. His distinguished visitors could travel from Newcastle to Morpeth, Scots Gap and Rothbury. It is a great pity that the line does not still exist as a scenic route. Perhaps it could become a footpath between two important National Trust properties.

Our route continues to Rothley crossroads, and turning southwards we view Rothley Crags and Castle, pass the shrunken village of Rothley and reach Oakford, where the Delf meets the Hart which passes under the road. At Oakford there was a water mill and another Rothley Mill to the east of the road. Both are now disused and the waters move on unimpeded to join the Wansbeck beyond Hartburn.

HARTBURN VILLAGE

This is a very pleasant settlement along the- west bank of the river. The houses are mostly built of stone, the more modern buildings in keeping with the old. There

are steep banks to the river and the western bank is covered with trees. To the west of the village there is an attractive walk to Garden House and in the village is a pathway down to the river. The lower path reaches the grotto, which Dr Sharpe had cut into the rock, with two rooms, one having a fireplace. These were for the use of bathers, who were able to reach the water under cover of a tunnel. There was prob-

Hartburn Grotto, used by Dr. Sharpe, vicar of Hartburn, as a changing place for bathers, with a tunnel to the river.

ably a dam to raise the level of the water which now flows over a rocky bed and is not very deep. Two niches above the entrance to the grotto once carried the figures of Adam and Eve.

Dr Sharpe (1748-1792) with the support of the village was responsible for the construction of the castellated building that provided the parish stable on the ground floor and the school and school-house above. The northern front looks like a castle and could be described as a "folly". From it are excellent views of the countryside and the river. Hereabouts the Devil's Causeway crossed the water, and Hodgson who lived here from 1833-1845, saw post holes for the timbers cut into the rock.

The Rectory is a fine building. It consisted of a Vicar's Pele or tower to which a mansion was added with extensions of several periods. At the east end of the long garden stands the Church of St Andrew.

Dowsing has indicated that there were earlier and smaller churches on the same site within the nave and chancel of the present structure. The earliest visible stonework seems to be of the Norman period, an aisleless church with possibly an apsidal east end. The tower has a band of Norman-like decoration below the top, and a number of roundheaded windows have been blocked. Double lancet windows were inserted and in the west wall a larger window, which is 13th century. The whole of the windowhead is monolithic ie carved out of a single piece of stone. There are a number of smaller monolithic heads in other windows, but no windows to the north, thus providing protection from the winds. It had a high pointed roof, indicated by marks on the east side of the tower. The slope continued down the aisle walls, which were later raised in height when flatter roofing was fixed.

The site is most attractive, overlooking the Hartburn and the graveyard is almost a garden with snowdrops, daffodils and bluebells in turn. Later the roses and other flowers are in bloom. It is well kept and there is a collection of grave

stones, many going back to the 18th century and further. Some of them carry curious carvings of the symbols of time – the skull, thigh bones and the hourglass. Thomas Whittell (1681-1731) is buried in the graveyard. Hodgson says of him – "He was employed in painting such heraldic and other tablets as are usually put up by authority in churches, in engraving inscriptions on tombstones and in other works of art and ingenuity." (Hodgson)

Hodgson's grave is at the east end of the church, dug into rock and covered with a medieval type of grave cover with a floriated cross. Another tombstone is that of Mephibosheth Goddard of Longwitton, who died in 1790.

The church is entered by a stone slated porch and the door within has attractive dogtooth ornament about it; there is a step down into the nave. The graveyard level has been raised by many interments, and in the nave are two large stone coffins on display. The tower arch has been blocked, and if the visitor turns about and looks down the nave into the chancel, it will be seen that there is a lack of alignment. One view (religious) is that it represents the head of Christ drooping on the cross, and the other (architectural) is that medieval masons made mistakes. The arcades of the nave have four bays with octagonal piers and moulded capitals. In the south aisle one capital has a ball ornament and the other carries a single fish. The chancel has lancet windows and a number of monuments. The sedilia have monuments within their arches – one to John Hodgson, Vicar and Historian, d. 1845 and his wife d. 1853, another to Richard Werge, priest who died in 1749 and finally Beilby

Hartburn Church, an interesting building, with monuments within and without. Hodgson's grave is at the east end of the church.

Porteous Hodgson, Vicar of Hartburn for 32 years, who died in 1889, aged 81. The oldest gravestone, of Frosterley marble, set in the floor is that of Sir Thomas de Errington 1302-1310. It carries the indent of a brass and you are asked 'Orate pro anima', to Pray for his Soul.

There is a very fine monument in white marble to Lady Bradford, who died on her way back from India in 1830. The sculptor was Chantrey and shows the figure of a lady reclining. Another to J H Atkinson of Angerton who died in 1873 is a white marble effigy with Christ and angels behind. The chest for the collection of money near the door of the church is said to be that of Cromwell, who stayed at Netherwitton in 1651. Out in the churchyard again we can see the Hart passes under the high arched bridge and makes its way through a wooded valley towards Angerton Broom House, where it joins the River Wansbeck below Meldon Park. From Hartburn Church there is a pleasant footpath across the fields to Angerton, and the road descends an avenue of laburnum trees, brilliantly golden when in flower.

ANGERTON HALL

Angerton Hall is secluded in woodland, overlooking the Wansbeck to the south. It was the work of John Dobson (1787-1865) who was responsible for the development of Bolam Park and Lake for Lord Decies. He is one of the most important of Northumbrian architects. He is best known for his work in Newcastle and for country houses built in classical style. Angerton shows he was not limited in his range. It is usually described as Tudor style or Gothic. Dobson carefully picked his site, south facing and sloping to a river. Woodland belts provided seclusion and shelter. The house was built in 1823, and the railway came forty years later.

Angerton Hall is L-shaped with a covered entrance near the re-entrant angle. The main fronts to the east and south overlook gardens. The immediate surrounding wall is a low balustrade. The gardens were later developed by Sir Edwin Lutyens. The fenestration of the house is regular with mullions and flat hood moulds. Though built in Tudor style, is dispenses with lavish and costly decoration. The chimneys are very restrained compared with true Tudor fashion.

MELDON PARK

Not very far away to the north and above the junction of the Wansbeck and Hart is Meldon Park. This too is in an elevated situation, south sloping and overlooking the river. It commands extensive views except to the north where the woods stand proudly. Meldon Park was designed by Dobson for Isaac Cookson. It was to be the centre for estates that had been purchased from Greenwich Hospital (formerly Derwentwater's). Dobson provided a water colour painting to show what the house would be like. It is square in shape and built in classical style – that is regular and all in proportion with no excessive ornamentation. The entrance portico on the west is supported by Ionic columns. The windows are deeply recessed and on the ground floor continue below the sill to ground level. Within is a spacious

entrance hall and a fine staircase. The rooms contain some attractive plasterwork and there are bay windows on the south front. There is a conservatory to the east of the house and to the north offices and stables. The gardens are beautiful. The date of Meldon was 1832, and there is more Dobson to follow along the Wansbeck.

Meldon Park is north of the old village of Meldon and Hodgson wrote – it "extends from the village of Meldon to the northern boundary of the parish: it is surrounded with a stone wall laid in mortar, which, till within the last 20 years was in many places 12 feet high, but has been uniformly reduced to about S feet. It was probably made by the Radcliffe family. Deer horns are frequently found here, one in particular, remarkable for its size was turned up by the plough 5 or 6 years ago, in the low wet ground to the south west of the bridge and is now in the possession of Mr Wailes one of the receivers of Greenwich Hospital. The Park Keeper's House an old grey building, on the southern banks of the river, though in a low and warm situation is raised high enough to give its tenant a supervisor's eye over nearly the whole area of the Park and in the arrangement of its chimney tops and mullions and weather mouldings of its windows, was, no doubt at the time it was built, a crack specimen of the architecture of the seventeenth century." (Hodgson)

Today the wall can be seen to its full five feet, and the Keeper's House is still there on the drive down to Meldon Mill, a very substantial structure belonging to the Cooksons and having fine stables and gardens. The fields crossed by a wooded Wansbeck are very attractive and Meldon Village is on rising ground to the south.

Hodgson tells us that Greenwich Hospital was making great changes before the Cooksons purchased the property. During the Napoleonic Wars (1793-1815) the price of corn made change from pasture to tillage very profitable, but it involved the construction of new buildings costing £7,400 and drainage £4,000. There was a threshing machine driven by water power. The farms were considered a model for the time, and 50 acres of land were planted with oak, ash, beech, elm, larch and fir. One hundred and forty acres of ancient woodland were improved by thinning. The old mill had been pulled down and replaced in 1788.

Meldon Church, dedicated to St John, stands on a hill to the south of the Park. It is a small church, originally dated to the 12th century and not much altered. The nave and chancel are as one and measure 20 feet wide and 60 feet long. It has a bellcote, restored in medieval style. Before 1736 it was in very bad repair without a roof, but it was repaired by the Dean and Chapter of Durham, and the incumbent wrote – "I myself purchased a decent pulpit and a reading desk and a full set of pews, with Dr Eden's money, out of a given over meeting house in Morpeth." (Hodgson)

The church was again restored in 1849, and a monument to Isaac Cookson, who died in Munich, was placed there (1851). At the west end of the church is the monument to Sir William Fenwick, who died in, 1652. He is shown reclining on his side, his cheek propped up by his hand. His residence was Meldon tower, which was there in 1415, and probably had a mansion added to it. But in Hodgson's time it had disappeared. "It stood at the corner of a hedge about 150 yards south east of

the church and partly in two fields, where there are strong remains of the walls of vaults or cellars 60 feet long and 15 feet wide." There were traces of other buildings south of the church.

In Meldon Church is an inscribed stone built into the west wall; previously it was in the floor. "Here lyeth the body of Mr Arthur Skinner, who was a faithful friend and servant of Sir John Swinburne January 27 1667." Sir John Swinburne stayed at Meldon 1667-1668 while Capheaton was being rebuilt. It indicates that Meldon was a considerable mansion, since the Fenwicks were a powerful family.

Strange gravestones in Meldon Churchyard, showing the symbols of time and human mortality – hourglass and bones.

MEG OF MELDON

A lot has been written about Margaret Fenwick, considered a witch in her later years. She died in 1631, and in the 17th century there was a fear of witches, with witch hunts and condemnations to death. All kinds of misfortunes were attributed to the machinations of evil old women, all kinds of habits and activities could be misinterpreted. Bad weather, failure of crops, sour milk, foul meat, aches and pains, illness and sudden death were attributed to witches. Legends grew up about Meg of Meldon, and MacKays of Morpeth printed a "New Penny History" with this title. Meg had a familiar called Zepna, who was a servant of the devil and got her into all kinds of crimes- successfully.

She was Margaret Selby, a member of another important family and married to

Sir William Fenwick. Their son, also William Fenwick, lived at Meldon. Margaret in her later years lived at Hartington Hall, another Fenwick residence. She was said to be very fond of money and miserly about it, secreting "treasure" in various places. Anything found in this way was considered to be the result of her hiding it. After her death she wandered nightly in search of her lost treasures. There was supposed to be a hidden underground way from Hartington to Meldon. The old stone slabs of the pavement were connected with it, and a "battling" stone at Hartington, which was for beating webs of cloth, had some special significance. An old picture found at Hartington showed Meg with a big round black hat tied down over the ears, a stuff gown upturned to the elbows and a ruff about her neck. There was also a picture of her and her husband at Ford Castle.

But in the legend she could take various forms and travel great distances. One place she visited was Newminster Abbey, where there is still a special stone coffin by which she sat. Water in it was supposed to cure warts. She ran over Meldon bridge in the form of a little dog. Sometimes she was a hare, and sometimes strange lights could be seen glinting in the water. The abutments of the old bridge are still there below the present one. Numerous bags of gold were found. The hoard in a bull's hide down Meldon Well was not recovered, but one day in the old school while the Master was out a bag of coins fell from the roof through the ceiling. The lads scrambled for them and we shall never know the dates on them. (Incidentally Mrs Jane Pye was executed at Goosehill, Morpeth for witchcraft in 1658.)

I think (for I have seen this) that the dog could be a large owl flying slowly along a hedge or wall and it would appear to be running it. Strange lights could be the phosphorescent glow of a decaying beech tree, the waters of Wansbeck providing the moving reflections. We also know that when peace was often lacking and banks were non-existent, people buried their valuables for security. It might be the result of a raid or civil war that often the treasure was not recovered by the owner. A hoard of medieval silver coins was found under the floor of the old tower at Fenwick (the origin of the Fenwicks). The building was being used as a stable and excavating the old floor revealed the hoard. It was thought to have been for a ransom to the Scots, but more likely to have been hidden from them. The same thing happened in the Wars of the Roses or the Civil War, when the winning side in battle would confiscate the property and valuables of the other. But coinage, gold, silver and jewellery could be hidden away and escape confiscation. Death in battle or exile might mean it was forgotten. So Meg of Meldon may explain some historical and archaeological problems.

Others can be explained by examining the landscape. Between Meldon Village and Meldon Park is a house called Clay House. Hodgson explained that here was obtained a special blue clay that was worked and sent to Gateshead for glasshouse pots. There were also, a little further down the river at Rivergreen, a number of pottery kilns. A spoil heap mound indicates where it was and nearby was Garden House. "The garden itself was one of the finest nursery grounds in the north and was occupied by one Walter Turnbull." (Hodgson).

Coal was also mined in this area for the kilns. The once impressive mill, stone-built and pantiled, has in recent years been demolished. The number of watermills that were once active along the river is surprising and used for a variety of purposes. It is a great pity that more of this non-polluting power is not used today. Hodgson wrote of Rivergreen "This is one of the lovely and lonely spots with which the sides of the Wansbeck abound. The mill, the river, the flowery haugh, the old orchard and its cosy and sheltered cottage – all these girt around with shaggy and wooded banks and enlivened with the miller and the woodman's families, form a panorama, which wants nothing but some picturesque accompaniments, as it once had in its patriarch Joshua Delaval and his fourscore goats and kids to make it a subject, by magic of some master's hand, worthy of blooming on canvas through the live long year." The picture and the photograph can capture what is by its nature ephemeral.

MOLESDEN

Molesden, the next hamlet along the way, shows how much things change. The farmhouse and buildings are being converted entirely to residences and other buildings are built for farm purposes. This area is attractive for the many hawthorn hedges that remain, and in summer the blossoms hang as thick as snow and the scent is sweet. The smoke of the railway has gone, but at times there is the acrid taste of oilseed rape with bright yellow flowers. Eastwards the road turning at right angles indicates that at one time West Coldside, Middle Coldside and East Coldside were a village. Middle Coldside has vanished, but the others remain and the road moves on to Mitford. Mitford Steads once had a water wheel to drive the machinery in the barn. Then this was replaced by a round house or gin-gan, ie a building to cover the horses as they went round and round to turn the machinery in the barn. The wheel-pit and gin-gan remain, but power is now provided by the tractor and electricity.

The area of the millpond can still be seen, and the small stream that fed the millpond moves on to join the Wansbeck at Mitford. It passes through a deep wooded ravine and emerges under a little old stone bridge to feed the moat of Mitford Castle. It may be that the older village of Mitford lay towards Mitford Steads and the name of Aldworth (old settlement) may indicate this. The exact location of Aldworth, which has disappeared entirely, is not known.

MITFORD

The road from Mitford Steads and Gubeon joins the Mitford Road, almost on the Wansbeck. Mitford Hall can be seen through the trees to the north, but our attention is taken by the embodiment of Mitford's medieval past – the Castle, which is very impressive.

It was the head of a barony and held in 1100 by William Bertram, who married a daughter of Guy of Balliol. He was the builder of the first castle on the site – a motte and bailey type. The place was well chosen, situated on a rocky ridge south

of the Wansbeck, which curves round it. It guarded one of the fords of Mitford, which was later replaced by the Foss Bridge. The Park Burn supplies water to the moat and still, when we have rain, makes the land about marshy. The ridge was modified to make the castle platform, with earth thrown up from the ditches. The motte or mound dominated the area of the bailey to the west and what was called the barmkin to the east. The first structures were timber, later replaced by stone. The main entrance at the west end has been destroyed by quarrying. Like Morpeth, Mitford Castle was destroyed 1215-1216 by King John in his war of revenge against the northern barons. But it was rebuilt and repulsed the attacks of the King of the Scots. In 1315 in the troubled time following the defeat of Edward II at Bannockburn, it was taken over by Gilbert de Middleton and his supporters. It was used as a centre for his pillaging raids and here he brought as captives Bishop Beaumont of Durham and his brother, hated as foreigners. They were held in Morpeth and Mitford castles till the ransoms were paid. Mitford Castle was recaptured in 1317 and Gilbert was taken and put to death. One of his supporters, Sir Walter Selby, recaptured it with the help of the Scots. There were further Scottish raids and in 1327, Mitford was described as "the site of a castle wholly burned". After this it was only used occasionally and not inhabited. It would need complete excavations to tell the story. In 1566 Lord Burgh sold the lands of Mitford to Cuthbert Mitford, but the Mitfords did not get the Castle till 1666. There had long been another residence – the Old Manor House.

The Castle became a romantic ruin, whether viewed from the Old Hall or the

Mitford Castle dates back to 1100, having many additions and alterations. It was abandoned after destruction by the Scots in 1318.

new one, built by Dobson. The castle enclosure became gardens and an orchard. In time they deteriorated and were invaded by the cattle. Before 1939, excavations took place, but they were never properly reported, and the finds were stored in a hut that became a war casualty. Mitford Castle is unique and should be properly excavated and maintained. As already mentioned it started as a motte and bailey castle. Then the motte was converted into a shell keep ie a strong wall was built all round it and protected within the bailey by a deep ditch. There were buildings within the shell keep, entered by a door on the east side. Still later in the 13th century a pentagonal tower was built within the shell keep – the only one of this shape in the country. This provided an extra command point to cover the fortifications. Most of it has disappeared and only the double vaults of the basement remain. They are entered by stone steps and at times were used as a prison. One unfortunate had carved on the stone steps the words "captivus morior" (I die a prisoner), and the date was during the Wars of the Roses. The vaults were built as store places or cellars. There are stone spouts to bring in the rain water which would be stored in lead or stone cisterns. The curtain wall on the east side of the keep has disappeared as far as the postern gate and tower. The south wall still stands to a considerable height, overlooking a ditch quarried in stone. The south west area has been quarried away in the last century to build the new hall. The gatehouse has been pulled down, but the area of the chapel can be picked out with some small gravestones. Hodgson thought a lot of bones there might be from a massacre, but it appears to be the cemetery. A chapel had been built over earlier walls and graves. There was also evidence of a hall,

Mitford Old Hall is in ruins. The central porch tower is dated 1637, but the building was much older.

which existed before the pentagonal tower was built over part of it. Since the decayed elm trees have been removed the site is much clearer and there is more to explore. From an arched opening in the north wall the area of the church, old hall and vicarage can be viewed. The Old Hall or Manor House succeeded the Castle as a residence and, like the castle, was plundered for building stone.

Mackenzie wrote in 1825 – "The old mansion house is seated near the river, at a short distance north of the castle. The kitchen is occupied by the gardener, but the greater part of the house was pulled down about 12 years ago by the present proprietor, who intended to erect an elegant mansion house on the opposite side of the river. The work at present is suspended: but a large quantity of excellent stone was prepared. It was procured from the bed of the River Font and is susceptible of as fine a polish as marble. An old tower, which forms the entrance into the mansion house, is still standing." It carries the arms of the family and bears the date 1637.

The old kitchen wing which still stands as a residence, was one wing of a quadrangular building constructed about a courtyard. Single walls still stand and the foundations of the building that stood behind the entrance tower. At one time a dog wheel to turn the spit could be seen in the kitchen as photographed by Canon McCleod. This can now be seen in Morpeth Chantry Museum. The building stands in a pleasant garden setting adjacent to the church with the river to the north. The residence is now private, but the Mitfords retained their old porch tower, which once ornamented the south front of the old mansion.

Mitford Hall was designed by John Dobson in 1823, replacing the Old Hall and castle. The Hall and lands after many centuries, no longer belong to the Mitfords.

The new house stands to the west and north of the Wansbeck. Dobson's plans were drawn as early as 1823, but building did not begin till 1827. An attractive site was chosen on the north slope of the Wansbeck. The approach was by a gated lodge and a long winding drive through trees and bushes. The stables are to the north of the house and the woodland provides shelter from the prevailing winds. The entrance to the Hall is by a western portico like Meldon, but with Doric columns. The building has regular classical features with projecting cornices and a balustrade at roof level. To the east is the conservatory. The setting amid gardens and woodland is most attractive. There are views of the church, the old hall and the castle, which Dobson landscaped as an eye catcher. Hodgson wrote – "The new Manor House ... is a very handsome square edifice built from designs of Mr Dobson. The beautiful white sandstone of which its outside walls are built is obtained from a stratum of rock which forms the bed of the Font. Great praise is due to the owner for choosing a stone, which is not only beautiful, but has every appearance of being indestructible to atmospheric agents. The site of the house is well chosen. This is a fertile and most delightful place." (Hodgson)

The Church also is attractively situated and is dedicated to St Mary Magdalene. The reason is that in 1307 Edward I granted the advowson of Mitford to Lanercost Abbey, which was devoted like himself to St Mary Magdalene. He stayed for some time at Lanercost, which had suffered from attacks by the Scots (as had Mitford). The church at Mitford has a history going back to Norman times.

There was a smaller church with an apsidal east end, but it was developed into a building of cruciform shape, with both north and south aisles. In Hodgson's time it seems it was in a ruinous condition. Part of the west end had been lopped and a poor bellcote built. The Norman arches of the south aisle had been built up and the roof was flat or nonexistent. Pevsner says that the north aisle disappeared in the 13th century, but Hodgson quotes a document (1764) – "The passage into the north aisle flagged, and the aisle itself replastered and whitewashed", (Hodgson) so it was there. He speaks of the north (or Pigdon) porch and the south (or Mitford) porch. These are the transepts. The chancel then was large and lofty, the structure mainly of the 13th century, although there is evidence of earlier building – for example the Priest's door. The east end has three lancet windows and the south has six, with slender buttresses on the outside.

In the 1870s the church was extensively rebuilt by Colonel Osbaldiston Mitford at a cost of £10,000. At the west end the nave returned to its full length and a 20 feet square tower was added with a spire. It contained a full peal of eight bells which could be operated mechanically to play tunes. The stout Norman pillars and arches of the south aisle were restored, but those of the north aisle were blocked. A beautifully carved reredos was set up in the chancel and Thomas Bowman Garvie of Morpeth painted frescoes above the chancel arch. By contrast is a rather crudely carved monument to Bertram Reveley of Throphill, inscribed thus –

Here lyeth Interred With –
in this Molde. A Generous and
Virtuous Wight. Whose

Dews Deserte Cannot be
Told, From Slender Skil Unto
His Right, He was descended
From a Race of Worshipful
Antiquities, Loved he was
In his Life-Space, of High
Eke of Low Degree. Rest
Bertram In This House of Clay
Reve'ley unto The Latter Day.
Below is his effigy, cut in low relief are further lines
Bertram to us so dutiful a Son,
if more were fit it should for
thee be done, who deceased
the 7th of October, Annon Domini 1622.

The church has some interesting registers and records.

"June 9th 1680. One of our bells is useless. No terrier (ie land book) of the glebe. John Davison, Roger Burke and Thomas Trumble for playing on the Lord's Day at bobbe hand ball presented. Our quire is out of repair."

Isaac Nelson 1759-1772 rebuilt the vicarage, but "as he was returning home from Morpeth on Friday 20th March 1772, he was drowned at the stepping stones at Mitford". (Hodgson)

At a time when bridges were lacking, how many more victims did the waters of Font and Wansbeck claim?

The crossings of the Wansbeck were important to the development of a settlement. Mitford as the head of a barony, had a market and fair which at one time was considered more important than Morpeth. As the waters of Font and Wansbeck united below Mitford they could be crossed by two fords, one over each river at Mitford thus reducing the danger.

The Bertrams had founded Brinkburn Priory and there was a direct road from Mitford to Brinkburn. They also granted lands to the Abbey of Newminster, which lay in between Mitford and Morpeth. However, when the Chantry Bridge was built at Morpeth in the reign of Edward I, this borough gained the advantage. There was a lot of through traffic during the Scottish Wars and so the Morpeth craftsmen flourished – the armourers, the smiths, the saddlers and masons especially. Mitford also lessened in importance when Bothal Castle was built. There seems to have been no industrial development.

In 1825 Mackenzie mentions a water-mill where blankets were made, but it failed and was converted into a snuff mill – the millstones used for grinding tobacco. The mill has recently been converted into a private residence, and the last industry has closed – George Brown's Saw-mills.

The power was provided by a steam engine named Bess which drove the saws.

The fuel for the fire of the engine was taken from other estates than Mitford, and the Browns made all kinds of timber products – fencing, carts, waggons, repairing the horse gins or engines. Watermills were also repaired. Brown's yard has been built upon – attractive houses near the rivers, and on the other side of the road emerges another strange looking building – a house which is thatched with Norfolk reed. The Plough, the public house, has been rebuilt since the time of Canon Macleod's photographs and the Granary restaurant added. The old smithy has been converted into a shop and the old fountain was restored by the Mitfords. St Cuthbert is supposed to have blessed the well, the waters of which could work miracles.

Above the bridge over the Font is Spittal Hill House. This is an attractively situated 18th century mansion, with later additions, built in fine stone and has beautiful views of Mitford. Spittal Hill is named after the medieval hospital of St Leonard founded by Sir William Bertram. Bones have been disinterred by gardening activities. There are splendid walks on or above the River to Morpeth and also along the Font to Dean House and Benridge.

Life in Mitford in the earlier part of the 20th century was recorded by Canon Macleod, for many years resident at Mitford and related by marriage to the Mitfords. He took all kinds of photographs of workmen, children at play and at school, the Mitford orchestra, the choir trip or Sunday School outing and the women at work in the fields. These photographs in the form of glass slides have been deposited at Northumberland County Record Office, and have often been reproduced in books. They are considered to be of the highest quality. It now becomes necessary for us to trace the route by which the waters of the Font arrive at Mitford and join the Wansbeck.

CHAPTER V: THE RIVER FONT, TRIBUTARY OF THE WANSBECK

The Font has its origins in the Harwood and Rothbury forests. The Rothbury forest was medieval, the Harwood forest is modern. The area is remote and at one time much of it was "moss" and rough pasture. The streams that combine to make the Font are the Fallowlees, Newbiggin and Blanch Burns. Their combined waters make the Fontburn Reservoir. The area contains a number of earthworks – at Manside Cross, Fallowlees and Ewesley.

At Greenleighton was a grange or farm of Newminister Abbey, where in medieval times farming was essentially the keeping of sheep. The grange had a tower or stone house for defensive purposes and a chapel.

Another stone house stood at Fallowlees, where once there was ironworking and leadmining. There is similar evidence at Redpath, a neighbouring farmstead. Sir Walter Blackett had a shooting box built which he called "Blackcock Hall." It was later burnt by gypsies. Fallowlees, in 1666, received the fugitive Scottish Covenanter, William Veitch and later his family. The Covenanters were hounded terribly in Scotland and had to find hiding places. Veitch wrote that "he removed his wife and two sons, William and Samuel in creels, from Edinburgh to a village called Falalies, farming a piece of land from Charles Hall who was owner of that place and village." (Hodgson) Veitch moved on to Harnham Hall and then Stanton Hall, where he was sought by Magistrates, but escaped.

An important development in the 1860s was the construction of a railway from Scots Gap to Rothbury. The permanent way passed to the west of Rothley Lakes to stations at Longwitton and Brinkburn. This resulted in some industrial development. There were large lime kilns near Rothley and limestone was quarried at Greenleighton and elsewhere.

There was considerable mining activity around Longwitton, Coldrife, Forestburn with ironworks at Brinkburn. Since there were passenger services there was considerable change to the rural community and a decline in horse transport. Cattle could be taken by train, passing the old assembly place at Donkin rigg.

FONTBURN RESERVOIR

The railway was specially important for the construction of the Fontburn Reservoir and Waterworks. The trains passed over the Fontburn valley on a lofty viaduct, which still stands though the railway is now disused. It was a most attractive route, but never profitable.

The supply of fresh water was an increasing problem to the ever growing urban areas and there was never enough. Tynemouth in 1898 obtained an Act of Parliament, authorising the construction of the Fontburn Reservoir. Good stone was available from Greenleighton and Ritton White House quarries, both of which are now closed.

The construction of the reservoir began in 1901 and was complete in 1908. For this work and servicing the industry a new village grew up with its own school and other facilities. In the course of time, with the work completed and later the decline of the railway, the settlement was reduced to a few houses and distant farmsteads. There was another small school at Rothley Shield West which was closed with the decay of local industry. The viaduct remains as do the old lime kilns and quarries below Ritton White House, which embodies a pele tower. The disused railway could be a pleasant walk through varied landscapes with distant heather hills.

Today the visitor can be surprised at the number of people gathered at the Fontburn Reservoir. The western end of the waters is a Nature Reserve. The Reservoir provides entertainment as well as the necessary supplies of water. In the dry summer of 1991, the waters were more than 10 feet below the full level and there was no overflow. In the past the Reservoir has been liable to flash flooding.

The River Font passes under the Alemouth or Corn Road into the valley of Nunnykirk, which is beautifully fringed with trees. The landscape, however, shows the scars of a great deal of mining and quarrying. There are a number of bell pit mounds in the fields and the walls of deserted houses.

Coltpark once had a school, and at one time with the Rittons belonged to the Abbot of Newminister. The Park was an enclosure in which the larger animals were kept – deer and cattle. In 1542 there was a stone house with an enclosure which, like the other Newminster lands in this area, belonged to King Henry VIII. Nunnykirk also came into the King's hands. The abbot of Newminister had here built a chapel, a defensive tower and other buildings.

Hodgson wrote at a time of rebuilding at Nunnykirk that old foundations were found and human bones were dug up. The owner was Mr Ordo "who is beautifying it with large additions to the old mansion house in a style of great elegance and simplicity, from designs and under the direction of Mr John Dobson of Newcastle, architect".

He added to the existing house quite successfully as Pevsner comments – "Very nobly Greek, with exquisite ashlar masonry and plenty of honeysuckle friezes."

In the centre is the rectangular hall with a gallery and a dome providing light. Portraits of Ordes are about the walls. The ceiling is tastefully decorated with plasterwork and neat metalwork surrounded the gallery. The entrance is by an Ionic pillared portico and a colonnade links the new structures across the front of the older house. The riverside front has rounded bay windows. The heavy horizontal rustication of the stonework confirms the connections of the old and the new. The hall is now used as a school for children with special needs. It is beautifully situated, in the valley of the Font attractive with trees and wildlife. I once saw an otter here.

NETHERWITTON

Unfortunately on the approach to Netherwitton from Ritton towards Folly House, there are the ugly gashes of opencast mining, which removes all archaeological evidence. There was mining here as "Coalhouses" indicates. Folly House

was the residence of the mines manager in the 1888 Directory.

"Baird, Thomas, bank manager, Nether Witton Colliery: h. Folly House." (Bulmer) But then, as today, the most important product was timber. There were a number of foresters and woodmen.

Joseph Green and William Green were timber merchants. Robert Sproat, wood dealer, had a saw mill and lived at Old Park. Joseph Lawton, woollen manufacturer, was at Netherwitton Mill and his son was his wool buyer, assistant overseer and clerk to the School Board, living at Factory House. The school was built in 1876 and 90 children then attended. Now it has been closed. The factory or mill was of great historical importance. Built in the 1780s by the Thorntons of Netherwitton

Netherwitton Mill was built in 1794 in country house style as a cotton mill, but soon converted to woollens and now to housing.

Hall, it was one of the earliest cotton mills in the country. It was built like a country mansion in classical style and worked by water power, not steam. In recent years it has been converted into a number of housing units, within the old structure, an award winning enterprise.

Netherwitton was formerly called Witton by the Waters, but it might well be called Witton in the Woods. The woodlands are particularly beautiful, but commercially viable. There is an attractive variety of trees, hard and soft woods, evergreen and deciduous. They are cut and replanted in sequence, a natural cover rapidly developing of flowers and bushes.

In the last century the woodlands were coppiced, providing wood for furniture and fencing. The bark of the oak trees went to the Morpeth tanneries.

The manor once belonged to Roger Thornton, a wealthy and successful Newcastle merchant, who helped to finance the building of St Nicholas and All Saints Churches in Newcastle. His elaborate memorial brass, now in St Nicholas Cathedral, records his death in 1429. He gained his wealth from trade but he was specially involved in lead mining, which produced silver as well as lead. In his will he made many gifts of lead to monasteries and churches. The priests also were handsomely paid to say hundreds of masses for his soul and for those of members of his family. "I commend my soul to the mercy of God and my body to be buried beside my wife in Allhallowes Kyrk of Newcastle." (Hodgson)

The Thorntons remained Catholic and in the Civil War supported Charles I. In the summer of 1650 Cromwell's army was at Netherwitton and he gave Lady Thornton protection "from violence to her person or any of her family or from taking away any of her horses, cattle or other goods whatsoever". There were 2,450 horse and others "all quartered for one night on the grounds of the Lady Thornton". (Hodgson) Much corn and hay was consumed or destroyed. The soldiers used hay for bedding in their tents. Lady Thornton was paid the sum of £96:5s:6d.

Netherwitton is situated near the Devil's Causeway, the Roman Road to Berwick, where Colonel Fenwick became Governor. This road was used in the

Netherwitton Hall, built about 1685, by Robert Trollope for Sir Nicholas Thornton, replacing an older strong house.

campaigns against the Scots of 1650-1651. Many prisoners were brought back after the Battle of Dunbar. The tower and mansion that stood in Cromwell's time was replaced by another handsome house built in the style of Robert Trollop. Some of the old stonework was included in the new house since an heraldic tablet with the Thornton arms above the north door bears the inscription "Anno Regis Edwardi Quinti" (In the year of Edward V ie 1483). This must be very unusual since the reign of the boy King was so short, murdered by his uncle, Richard, Duke of Gloucester. It may well be that this was the stair tower of the older house, like those at Witton Tower and Stanton, further down the Font.

Pevsner writes of Netherwitton Hall as "in the style of Trollop" and gives a date for its building as about 1700, after Trollop's death. But Wilkes thought it was built by Trollop and Hodgson says quite definitely it was his work. "The present house was built by Robert Trollop, the architect of Capheaton and of the town hall in Newcastle. It is of white freestone now weathered and grey: of three stories, with a flat roof and open battlements on the east, west and south fronts, the last of which is about 43 feet long and contains 21 windows. The north front looks into the yard of the offices and has two tower like offsets for staircases ..." (Hodgson)

There was a priest's hide within the walls, where Lord Lovat is supposed to have hidden after the 1745 rebellion. Hodgson continues – "The situation of the house is remarkably sweet and agreeable. From the west the Font steals past it, through woody and sheltering banks."

Witton Tower is a strong house, dated 1608, and built by a Thornton of Netherwitton. It once contained a Catholic Chapel.

Close by are the chapel of St Giles and the vicarage. The old village which lay to the south of the Hall, was removed to the other side of the Font, where the old cross with a date 1698 can still be seen. There are sheltered gardens to the west and the park surrounding the house is enclosed by a strong stone wall. The property came by marriage from the Thornton to the Trevelyan family. There was a Raleigh Trevelyan in Hodgson's time and there is a Raleigh Trevelyan there today.

The village is very attractive, especially from the bridge where the Ewesley Burn, having made its way from Rothley Lakes, joins the Font, which flows southwards before turning eastwards towards Shelley and then to Longshaws Mill. Northwards is Witton Shields, a tower house of the Thorntons – Nicholas Thornton built it in 1608, as inscribed on the door-head.

STANTON

The Font meanders through woodgirt banks to Stanton, where the water mill has disappeared. A farm lane leads towards Longshaws, where a Roman camp and fortlet have been revealed by aerial photographs.

Stanton Hall stands on the hillside, where once was a much larger village. This was shown by buried walls, a graveyard and chapel. Stanton tower stood there in the reign of Henry VI, and to this was added a Jacobean Hall. Later still in the 18th century a hall in classical style was added. It belonged to the Fenwick family, who held extensive lands. Their numbers included both strong protestants and Catholics. Colonel Fenwick was a strong supporter of Cromwell, whereas Sir John Fenwick of Wallington was put to death for treason to William III in 1696. In 1677 Veitch the Covenanter moved from Harnham Hall to Stanton Hall where he was received by "old Mr Fenwick and his lady". Three daughters were born to Veitch at Stanton, bringing the total of his family to ten. Scarcely had he arrived when the Magistrates were after him. They broke down the doors but he managed to hide in a hole in the lining of a big window. The house was searched from top to bottom without success. However in January 1679 he was caught and taken to Morpeth gaol, where he was held prisoner for 12 days. Later he wrote his memoirs. These were troubled times for Non Conformists as John Bunyan discovered in Bedford Gaol.

There was extensive coal mining in the Stanton area, as well as quarrying and lime burning. Evidence of these activities is still visible. Hodgson wrote – "Modern alterations have so defaced the tower which John Corbet occupied, that few traces of it are now observable: and the sashed and stoned mullioned windows, put in it by the Fenwicks, are patched with boards, or bundles of clouts and straw, or are open to the owls and daws. It is not, however, entirely tenantless. A person who earns a livelihood out of its sunny and well walled gardens, lives in part of it: a little shop is kept in another: a third portion of it is converted into a poorhouse: and the rest of the rooms are either unoccupied or only occasionally used as granaries. Some of the rooms are wainscoted with high panels and broad tiles painted in imitation of marble: and others hung with tattered tapestry. Many of the offices and

penthouses have been removed." Now the old ivy has been removed and the roof restored to the Fenwick building. It is an attractive garden centre with a shop and tea rooms. It is possible to speculate on the periods of alteration – the windows, the chimneys, the stonework and the old stair turret. Eastwards from Stanton and on top of rising ground is Beacon Hill. It is now covered with trees, but was formerly a great vantage point. The land extends widely in all directions and eastwards the sea glints in the sun and ships can be seen. Beacons were lit to warn the populace of the danger of a Scottish foray or in 1588 the coming of the Spanish Armada.

In a field near Stanton House is Clavering's Cross, a memorial to one who fell, it is said, at the hands of the Scots. This is what actually happened. On 22 November 1572 Sir Cuthbert Collingwood, the sheriff Robert Clavering and his brother William together with their wives and friends were returning from Newcastle after attending celebrations connected with Queen Elizabeth's accession. As they rode across the moor north of Morpeth they were attacked by a group of 10 to 15 soldiers from Berwick under the command of young William Selby of Branxton, son of the Deputy Warden of the East March. During the struggle that followed, Sir Cuthbert was shot in the stomach and William Clavering, the sheriff's brother, was killed. Fearing for his life Selby fled. Later several of the soldiers were tried, but only convicted of manslaughter. There seems to have been something of a family feud.

From Stanton the Font flows southwards and to the west on the Nun Burn is

Nunriding Hall, consisting of a pair of five bay houses. The one on the left is 17th century and the fuller right house is 18th century.

Nunriding Hall. Its name indicates that it was a clearing of woodland and it is still rather remote, reached by a winding lane with high hedges. The house and land once belonged to the Fenwicks and the bridge over the burn carries the date 1745 and the name of Robert Fenwick. The hall is 18th century in the classical style. It appears as a double house each having five upper windows and four lower windows with central doors, all with pronounced jambs. The situation is very attractive.

The River Font descends into a very deep valley, covered by tall trees. In this area there was both a quarry and a coal mine. The workings were once wrecked by the flooding of the river. The stone was good for tombstones.

Newton Underwood, the next village, was once much larger and contains a few stone houses. A farm house at the east end has an arch on thick walls, which might be the remains of a tower. "The place where it stands was called Old Walls, and in digging every way around it, strong foundations of buildings are still found." (Hodgson)

A hollow way, an ancient road, leads down to Lightwater and a small stream makes its way to join the Wansbeck. The Font continues to wind through wooded banks between Newton Park and Newton Mill to join the Wansbeck below the Mitford Bridge.

There was a bridge here 200 years ago, but at that time the Morpeth road had to cross two fords – High Ford and Low Ford before reaching Morpeth. By about 1830 new stone bridges had been built and the road was not so difficult. Between Mitford and Morpeth are modern waterworks, where water is taken from the river and processed. A weir maintains the level of the water and the river, after the fall, continues over its rocky bed, still overhung by trees. There are sluices and channels to take water to the Abbey Mills. One ran directly across the fields to the Abbey itself and can still be traced. The other is still in service, supplying the more modern Abbey Mills. Both are now residential, but still have the use of water power if necessary.

CHAPTER VI: NEWMINSTER ABBEY AND MORPETH

Newminster Abbey is situated between Mitford and Morpeth and appears a most attractive location, but when the Abbey was founded in 1138 it may well have been an unattractive area. The original Cistercian monks came here from Fountains Abbey in Yorkshire. A visitor to Newminster today will find it difficult to imagine what a splendid church was here. From 1536 it was despoiled by Henry VIII, whose agents took away its treasures and stripped the lead from the roof. Some of its timbers and stone were taken for military purposes and afterwards, over the centuries, the inhabitants of Morpeth helped themselves to the stone. It became a large quarry and the buildings were reduced to the foundations. The robbers had no use for carved stone or stone from windows and arches, which were left lying. It is from these that the quality of the buildings can be visualised. At one time only the ivy covered arch of the north door stood above ground, but in the early years of this century the abbey was excavated by Sir George Renwick. Much of the arcading was re-erected to form the squares of ornamental gardens, which could be viewed from his house above. At times they were open for the public to visit. It is a great pity that the area could not be developed in the fashion of Carlisle Park. The old ash trees that grew up on the site have rotted after 400 years, but one remains like a ghost. Nature is returning the land to what it was originally – the thorns are growing apace with the brambles and the wild roses. It is a haunt of birds and wild animals – the cattle are kept out and the visitor finds it hard to explore. It is worthwhile to walk up the hillside on the footpath for a general view of the area and other parts of Morpeth.

The Abbey site within the enclosing fence was excavated in the 1960s to establish an accurate plan, especially of the church. It was found to be large, measuring 254 feet in length. There was a square-ended presbytery to the east, two transepts each with three chapels and a nave of nine bays. A Galilee was added to the west end of the church in the 15th century. Buttresses had been added to give extra support. The buildings about the cloister were investigated. On the west side were the lay brothers quarters and on the east side the chapter house with the monks dormitory. The south range of kitchen and dining room was not explored. Remains of buildings extended beyond the fence. Running from west to east across the abbey was the drainage channel, which was some five feet high and two feet wide. It was well constructed and old inhabitants of Morpeth, who knew it, had all kinds of theories about it – "a secret tunnel" leading to the castle. From the higher viewpoint of the path some idea of the monastery can be obtained. The fishponds and the route of the water leading to them, can still be picked out. It is worthwhile looking at a plan of Fountains Abbey (the mother) and Roche (the daughter) to get the idea of the complete plan of Newminster.

Ranulph de Merlay, after a visit to Fountains Abbey, decided in 1138 to found and endow the Abbey of Newminster. It was soon attacked and severely damaged by the Scots, but rebuilt (Ranulph said in his charter) "for the health of myself, of

my wife, my sons, my lords and all my friends and for the souls of my father and mother, my forefathers and friends of all the faithful that are dead ..." (Hodgson)

The de Merlays and other important people were buried in the Abbey. Some of the stone coffins can still be seen on the site. St Robert, formerly of Fountains, was the first Abbot and the present Catholic Church was dedicated to him. He was born about 1100 at Gargrave in Yorkshire and studied in Paris, where he wrote a treatise on the psalms. He joined the monks at Whitby, but became one of the founders of Fountains in 1132. He then became Abbot of Newminster. He was distinguished by his zeal for prayer and poverty. His collections of prayers and meditations survived him in the library. In 1147 his monks accused him of excessive familiarity with a pious woman.

He was cleared of the charge and St Bernard, abbot and founder of Citeaux (origin of the Cistercians) gave him a girdle, which he kept at Newminster for healing the sick. Buried at first in the Chapter House, Robert was later translated to the church. Miracles were performed at his tomb, and one specially mentioned is of a monk who fell from a ladder to the floor while whitewashing the Chapter House and was unharmed. St Robert's Feast is 7 June.

During the excavation of the 1960s, a very valuable medieval buckle was discovered. Was this from the girdle of St Robert or a visitor?

The white monks renounced all luxury. They denied themselves cloaks, furlined boots, drawers, warm bedclothes and combs for the hair, just as they denied their abbey churches stained glass in the windows, gold and jewelled vessels for the altar, silk and embroidery and fine linen for vestments and hangings and human and animal figures in their stone carving. They had no processions, no litanies, little chanting and few psalms. They had the simplest of ceremonial and all their abbeys were dedicated to St Mary the Virgin. St Bernard wrote – "You will find in the woods something you never find in books" and "stones and trees will teach you a lesson you never heard from masters in school."

The sheep of their granges, tended by the lay brothers, were kept for wool not meat and after shearing time the bales of wool might be piled in the undercroft vaults at Newminster, ready for use locally or further afield.

Kings stayed here, and in 1503 Princess Margaret Tudor stayed on her way to Scotland to marry James IV. In 1515 she was back in Morpeth with a baby daughter, staying at the Castle. In 1603 her great grandson James VI of Scotland became James I of England.

MORPETH

Mark Akenside (1721-1770) often visited Morpeth.
"O ye Northumbrian shades, which overlook
The rocky pavement and the mossy fells
Of solitary Wansbeck's limpid stream:
How gently I recall your well known feats

Beloved of old and that delightful time,
When all alone, for many a summer's day,
I wandered through your calm recesses, led
In silence by some powerful hand unseen."
from *"Pleasures of the Imagination."*

The history of Morpeth begins with the Norman Conquest. Place name experts consider that its name, like Newcastle's first appears at this time. Morpeth, the first part of which comes from the French word mort (death), is taken to mean "murder path." Early roads in the area would converge and go down to a ford over the river, a place where persons might be waylaid and murdered. The possibilities are that places such as Kirkhill and Stobhill were the names of the early settlements.

Aerial photographs have revealed something like a dozen settlements in the Morpeth area. They appear as crop marks, which show enclosures with ditches and hut circles within. Nothing is visible on the ground. One site at Gubeon was excavated in advance of open cast mining, and proved to be a Romano-British settlement. There are sites on the golf course and on Park Farm. Indications are that there was a hill fort in this area, near the railway viaduct.

After the Norman Conquest Morpeth was granted by the King to William de Merlay and it became the head of a barony, the administrative centre of a large estate, which included Ulgham, Hepscott, Shilvington, Twizell, Saltwick, Duddo, Clifton, Stannington, Shotton and Blagdon.

William constructed the first castle of Morpeth on what is now called Ha' Hill. Here was a natural mound, which was altered by digging ditches and piling the earth higher into a motte (French = hill or mount). Round it were built timber palisades and wooden buildings were erected within the enclosure. It was constructed at first for protection against the conquered English, but in fact we hear of it in 1095 when it was being used in a rebellion against King William Rufus. It is not certain whether the castle stayed long on this site, for it was moved to the present site over the Postern Burn where the broken walls and gatehouse still stand.

The church of St Mary's was built on this same ridge some distance from the castle. The only sensible explanation seems to be that the settlement lay between the church and the castle, between the Church Burn and the Postern Burn. The first church dates back to the Norman period or earlier.

Morpeth Castle and town were burnt in 1216 after a savage attack by King John, incensed after a rebellion of barons forced him to sign Magna Carta. Roger de Merlay was one of the rebellious barons. He had obtained a charter from Richard I, who was raising money for his crusade. Roger paid a fine of 20 marks and two palfreys for the privilege of having a fair and market at Morpeth. This was the sign of borough status and meant that the burgesses of the town had some share in their own government. Tolls could also be taken and the ordering of the market could be controlled. The Lord (de Merlay) still had supervisory powers and could take "prizes" of bread, ale and other products to be paid within 40 days.

The burgesses were responsible for the erection of the Chantry Bridge in the reign of Edward I. It was most important for crossing the river at a time when there was much movement of men and materials between England and Scotland, especially when the wars came. It was a prosperous time for the crafts, and tolls could be levied for the maintenance of the bridge and the chantry chapel. Services were held for travellers and for townspeople in the new town, who found it some distance to travel to St Mary's. The De Merlays had developed a 'new town' to the north of the river as "Newgate" and "Newminster" indicate. It was carefully planned with burgage tenements on either side of the street. The houses were on the street front and the tenements stretched back to the river or Cotting Burn. A burgage was a long narrow strip on which extra buildings could be erected with garden, orchard and paddock. The townspeople might keep some animals near home. The open fields were held in common. Each person had a share or stint in them. The animals were herded together on the common under the supervision of a herdsman or shepherd.

The Subsidy or Tax Roll of 1296 lists the following taxpayers of the Borough of Morpeth:–

Reginald the forester: Robert the fuller: Robert of Hepscott: Robert, son of Alred: Adam of Buston: Robert the cobbler: Anges Crampe: William the weaver: John Halver: William of Newburn: John Sture: Alexander the cobbler: Robert of Alnwick: William Palmer: Richard of Gilling: Thomas Boule: John Pantill: Ralph of the booth: Alan of the garden: Robert the salter: Master Adam the clerk: Thomas of Coniscliffe: Adam the forester.

The 12 jurors of Morpeth also paid the tax. They were:–

Roger the fisherman: John the forester: Patrick of the booth: Richard son of Adam: Master Walter the Clerk: Richard the glover: Richard Hall: William of Roxburgh: Richard the smith: Ralph Culling: Robert son of Peter: Robert Stute.

These 35 taxpayers were only a small proportion of the male population. The list illustrates how surnames were derived – from fathers, from occupations and places. All these would have used the bridge and the Chantry chapel, where Master Adam (the Rose) was the priest. Master Walter was presumably connected with St Mary's Church. By this time after Roger de Merlay the Third died in 1271, the Lord of the Manor was William of Greystock, a Cumbrian knight, who married the heiress Mary de Merlay. His headquarters tended to be Greystoke in Cumbria. This family held Morpeth till 1487, when Ralph Lord Greystock died. His son, Sir Robert, had died before him and his heiress was his granddaughter Elizabeth, who married Thomas Lord Dacre of Gilsland. From his time we have a copy of the constitution of Morpeth. It was entitled "The Corporation of the Bailiffs and Burgesses of the Borough of Morpeth".

There were seven grouped companies or trade guilds, which provided both electors and members of the local government. They were:–

The Merchants and Tailors: The Tanners: The Fullers and Dyers with Carvers

and Hatters: Smiths, Saddlers and Armourers: The Cordwainers: The Weavers, and the Skinners, Glovers and Butchers.

The officials of the companies were aldermen and each company had its own rules and a box for documents and funds. The town treasury called "the hutch" was a heavy wooden box with seven locks and seven keys. It could only be opened when seven aldermen of seven companies were present.

The companies selected two bailiffs, a sergeant at mace, two fish and flesh lookers, two ale tasters, two bread weighers and four constables. The bailiffs were head officers of the corporation. The lord of the manor or his steward had final supervision. The sergeant at mace was the town crier and responsible for summoning persons to meetings and to the courts of law. The mace, which bears the date 1604 was presented to the borough by William Lord Howard of Naworth Castle, Cumbria, who married Elizabeth, the Dacre heiress.

The Howards were one of the most powerful and important families in the country, the head being the Duke of Norfolk. The Cumberland branch acquired the title of Earl of Carlisle from King Charles II, who confirmed Morpeth's Charter in 1662. A copy of this is kept in the Town Hall, along with the treasures of the borough.

The Town Hall, or earlier the Toolbooth, was the meeting place for justice, administration and elections. There is a map from the time of Lord William Howard (1603) which gives a very good picture of the lay-out of the town and the surrounding fields, indicating the demesne land which belonged to Lord William. "Belted Will", as he was called, was famous in his time and his accounts give details of his interests in Morpeth and the payments made to him. Most profitable were the mills which had to be used by local people, whether for grinding corn or fulling cloth. The manorial corn mill stood on the site of St George's Church. The tunnel of the mill race passes underneath the church floor and joins the Cotting Burn at the corner of the Old Red Bull. There was a fulling or wauk mill powered by the same water at the bottom of Tommy's Field. Another mill – East Mill – has been rebuilt several times and still stands. The windmill which was situated at Cottingwood in what are now the grounds of the High School, was wantonly demolished.

The 1603 map shows buildings on the castle site other than the gate-house, but the clock tower is not shown. The main streets – Bridge Street, Oldgate and Newgate – are shown with their houses and burgages, concentrated within the loop of the river.

Leland, in the reign of Henry VIII, had visited Morpeth after the Dissolution of the Monasteries. He wrote – "Morpith is a market towne XII long miles from NewCastle. Wansbeke a pratyrryver rynnithe the syde of the towne. On the hethar syde of the river is the principall church of the towne. On the same syde is the fayre castle standing on a hill, longinge with the towne to the Lord Dacre of Gilsland. The towne is longe and metely well builded with low howysys; the

stretes pavyd. It is a far fayrar towne than Alenwike. Morpith Castle standythe by Morpith towne. It is set on a highe hill and about the hill is moche wood. The towne and castle belongeth to the Lord Dacors. It is well mayntayed."

Thomas, Lord Dacre, fought at Flodden in 1513, and he discovered the body of James IV on the field of battle. In 1515 he received at Morpeth Castle James's widow Queen Margaret, Henry VIII's sister. She had married the Earl of Angus, but was expelled in 1515 and gave birth to a daughter at Harbottle Castle. She was brought to Morpeth in a litter and stayed at the Castle. In 1503 she had passed by on her way to marry James IV; she had stayed at Newminster Abbey. Leland had seen where was "New Minster Abbaye of White Monks, plesant with watar and very farye wood about it", but no more a place of the religious.

William, Lord Dacre, a Warden of the Marches, on occasion kept prisoners at Morpeth Castle. He was accused of incompetence by his enemies in that a notorious border thief, Cokes Charlton, was not sentenced and escaped to do untold damage. Dacre in his defence said that no-one would testify against Charlton, and some Tynedale men came by night, broke into the prison where the felons were and set them free. He was acquitted, but his case illustrates the problems of a man of authority on the Border.

On 14 December 1523 one of the orders for Morpeth, confirmed by Thomas Lord Dacre prohibited playing at "dyce, cardes or other unlawful games, but onely betwixt the feaste of St Thomas the appostle before Christenman (December 21st) and the daye of the Epiphanye (January 6th)" (Hodgson) the fine would be one shilling each time. One half was to be paid to the lord of the manor, and the other put into the "common chest".

Since the town was subject to Scottish raids despite the nightlywatches, rules of the craft guilds forbade the taking of Scottish apprentices. Morpeth was always a market for cattle, until quite recently, and an important industry was the tanning of leather. For this purpose large quantities of oak bark were needed, and some accounts have been kept showing the places where oak grew. For example:- June 2 1568 Michael Fenwick of Stanton, the bark of 100 oak trees £3:5s. Sept. 20 1607 to William Lord Howard 520 oak trees growing in the East Park, Morpeth £510. May 20 1628 Nicholas Thornton, John & Anthony Radcliffe of Netherwitton, bark of 600 trees growing in the East woods of Langshaws, for £50.

In 1683 the Tanners Company purchased "all the barque lying in the Great Hall of Bottle". (Hodgson) Henry Cavendish, second Duke of Newcastle, had allowed his grandmother's (Catherine Ogle) castle at Bothal to be used as a store, for oak bark. He had suffered severely during the Civil War as a leading Royalist general.

The amount of bark needed indicates the amount of work done by the butchers, skinners and tanners, and also the extent of the cattle market. Hodgson wrote "The weekly sale of oxen here has now for many years been upwards of 200 and of sheep and lambs 2,500, which are chiefly reared and fed in Northumberland and Scotland and consumed within the limits of the trade and ports of Tyne and Wear.

Part of them go as far as Leeds and Manchester: and when the demand for fat cattle is brisk in the South, considerable quantities are purchased here for the London market". This was at a time when cattle had to be driven to market, before transport was provided for them.

Edmund Bogg in his A Thousand Miles of Wandering in the Border County gives a dramatic picture – "On market days and fairs, Morpeth is aroused from its slumbers and it is very curious to watch the humble and jumble of humanity. At such times herds of shaggy cattle and droves of sheep are huddled in the streets, horses are trotted hither and thither to show off their paces: dogs are heard barking and yelping furiously: old cattle drovers – unique specimens of humanity – shuffle before our eyes like the sole survivors of a bygone generation, each carrying a stout stick, whooping, gesticulating and yelling at the pent up cattle, forming a veritable pandemonium. Cumbrous waggons, drawn by powerful horses, lumber slowly through the streets, vehicles of various descriptions containing farmers, their wives and daughters roll up to the various inns for the occupants to alight: and thus they come and the town grows into a ceaseless uproar of traffic and bargaining". (Bogg)

In 1822 there are recorded 34 Inns, Taverns and Public Houses as well as eight wine merchants and several brewers, so thirsty visitors and residents could be well supplied. There were eight blacksmiths in the town, seven coopers and eleven boot and shoe makers with five clog and patten makers; 25 butchers competed for trade, 18 grocers, seven bakers and 19 shopkeepers and dealers in sundries. Likewise there were 15 gardeners and seedsmen, nine milliners and dressmakers and 15 tailors.

It is appropriate that the Bridge Chantry at Morpeth, the old medieval chapel established by the craft guilds and burgesses in the time of Edward I, should now be the tourist information centre and a place of sale for various hand-made articles.

EXPLORING MORPETH ON FOOT

The story of Morpeth's development can be best explored on foot, and the **Bridge Chantry** is the place to start. Established for some 700 years, it has had a chequered history and more than once has come near to destruction. More than the castle or the churches, it symbolises the spirit of Morpeth – also being the Museum of the Northumbria Pipes, it echoes to music as it once echoed the priest intoning his Latin masses and the choir boys chanting their medieval Latin, learnt by repetition when where were no books to read. The ford was always dangerous but the bridge provided a safe passage at any time, until the arrival of modern traffic.

The Chantry chapel was built in the reign of Edward I. In 1296 Master Richard of Morpeth, Rector of Greystock, was granted a licence to found a chantry in "the chapel built in honour of All Saints, near the bridge of Morpeth". Here "divine services might be performed for the health of his own soul and for those of his father and mother, and of all benefactors of them himself and the said Lord (Greystock)". It was in the patronage of the burgesses and commonalty of Morpeth, who granted

The Chantry was connected with the medieval bridge, demolished after the Telford Bridge, on the right, was constructed in 1831.

it for life to Adam, called the Rose, of Morpeth "on the condition of his doing divine services in it, for the good of their predecessors and of the benefactors of the bridge and Chapel and of all the faithful departed out of this life". He was keeper of the bridge and chapel and according to the Commissioners of Henry VIII a grammar school was kept there for "the erudition and bringing up of children". (Hodgson)

In the Chapel there was another chantry in honour of the Virgin Mary and there were images both of Her and Jesus Christ, before which wax candles were regularly burned. Masses and prayers for the dead were the most important medieval service provided by the priests. With the Reformation, in Henry VIII's reign, these practices were condemned as superstitious. Henry VIII intended, and his son Edward VI enforced the dissolution of the Chantries. However, those that had provided a continuous service, such as a grammar school, could be reprieved. In 1547 Commissioners reported "Forasmuch as it appears that a grammar school has been continuously kept in Morpeth, we therefore, have assigned that the said grammar school in Morpeth shall likewise continue".

In 1541 a deed indicated that Sir Thomas Husband, a priest, kept a school and taught the children of the burgesses and inhabitants free of charge, but he could charge other scholars. If the revenue of chantry lands did not make a sufficient salary, the burgesses were to make it up to £6:13s:4d.

On 12 March 1552, a charter of Edward VI established in Morpeth the Royal

Grammar School, which took his name, and it remained in the Chantry buildings until 1846. The school was endowed with the lands of the two chantries in Morpeth and one at Netherwitton. The Netherwitton lands later led to a prolonged legal dispute with the Thorntons of Netherwitton, resulting in the payment of £15,000 which made possible the building of a new school on Cottingwood to replace the Chantry.

The Chantry Chapel was originally quite a large building, cruciform in shape. On its road side can be seen the arch of the north transept (which was filled in), the priest's door and the long lancets of medieval windows. The new school from 1552 assembled in the western part of the chapel, and the chancel or eastern part continued in use for religious services. In the 18th century the chapel was extended on the south side by the river, thus doubling the width of the chancel area to 42 feet. Its length is about 64 feet and that of the school about 42 feet within the walls. The western bell cote carried a bell, which belonged to the Chapel of Our Lady and was inscribed "Ave Maria, Gratia Plena, Dominus Tecum" (Hail Mary, Full of Grace, God be with you). This bell now reposes in retirement at the latest school on Cottingwood, where the active bells are electrical.

There is a great contrast in style and stonework of the medieval and later structures of the Chantry. MacKenzie (1825) wrote – "At the north east end of the bridge, and fronting the river, is a very handsome modern built chapel of white freestone. The grammar school which was founded by Edward VI, is kept in the west part." (MacKenzie) The old structure here remained, only the windows were enlarged and the original entrance built up. It was still possible to see the foundations of the demolished transept. The chapel had galleries to the north and west to provide extra seating. Services were held regularly here as well as at St Mary's Church. The chapel was near the heart of the town, and we are told that on sunny summer Sunday afternoons many of the congregation slept through the sermons. The chapel extension was well provided with large windows like a country house with two at the east end and five along the south wall. They are tall, symmetrical and regular with pronounced stone surrounds and Georgian glazing bars. The top of each window is arched in shape and the glazing bars are made to cross in what might be called a Gothic fashion. The upper windows at the east and west ends are strangely oval in shape, instead of the expected round. Pevsner wrote – "To the E. two gables with heavily arched coupled windows and oval windows above, all the detail severe in the Vanbrugh taste." (Pevsner)

Vanbrugh had designed Seaton Delaval and, for the Earl of Carlisle, Castle Howard. In Morpeth he designed the Town Hall, 1714, so he may well have influenced the style of the Chantry extension. Inside, the south wall was replaced by two round arches with columns almost like the bridge. The area of the south transept was covered by the new building, which is still well lighted. In 1966, the west end of the building was opened as a museum and the first exhibition included Girtin's picture of the Chantry and Bridge (1802), now housed in the Laing Gallery. In 1983, some years after the mineral water factory moved out and after extensive renovation, a Tourist Information Office was opened on the ground floor.

In due course the south chapel became a craft sales centre and the upper floor was developed as a Bagpipe Museum.

The important collection of bagpipes made by W A Cocks (1892-1971) and left to the Society of Antiquaries of Newcastle, was transferred from the Black Gate Museum to Morpeth.

There are two exhibition rooms and the visitor is supplied with earphones which enable him or her to listen to a particular type of pipe music as the instrument itself is approached. There are both examples of the real musical instruments and pictures for illustration. We are informed that in Chaucer's time, the bagpipes illustrated were considered by some to be "crude, bawdy instruments". The merry miller of the Canterbury Tales, was a music man of this type. Medieval illuminated manuscripts show shepherds piping to their sheep. Northumbrian shepherds produce many fine pipers. There was a variety of local bagpipes, but "Only the Northumbrian small pipes servive as a sole example of the English bagpipe", which is bellows blown. There are three Scottish types – the long or Highland bagpipes are best known and used for military music. Here the piper produces wind by blowing directly into the bag.

A series of bagpipes from different countries is shown. In the western part of the Bagpipe Museum is a meeting place for pipers. Local pipers are depicted and the places where they hold their meetings. Pictures of former pipers include the notorious James Allan of the eighteenth century. His father was a piper and his mother was a gypsy. He suffered from the wanderlust – joining the army and then deserting. The first Duchess of Northumberland played her part in maintaining the Northumbrian pipes, and took her pipers to London. James Allan was one of them, and there were many others who made a name for themselves. In recent years there has been a great resurgence of piping and classes held to instruct in making the music and making the pipes. A set of pipes is very much an individual instrument. Tapes can be bought in the Museum as well as music heard, making it a very pleasant place to visit.

The visitor is able in these upper rooms to examine the structure, the stonework and the timber work of the museum. The long blocked lancet window on the north side can be seen, showing how wide it was splayed to increase the inlet light. On the south side light floods in from the large 18th century windows. It is also possible to look out of these windows to view local sites – St George' Church, the Telford Bridge, the Court House, the river, the castle and houses.

Between the Chantry and the river is an enchanting Tudor-type garden, with formal box-edged borders. Above the waters, which once provided power for it, is Oliver's Mill. The pier of the medieval bridge provides a look back to the Chantry, a look ahead to the castle in a dominant position and a view along the river, the cutwater showing how the course of the river has altered. Looking the other way, the picture is the magnificent Telford Bridge erected in 1831 to take the place of the medieval bridge.

The Chantry Bridge, showing the medieval pier and the bellcote of the Chantry.

The Chantry Bridge consisted of two arches – the northern one spanned 51½ feet and rose 11½ feet. The southern arch spanned 51½ feet also and rose 13½ feet. The width of the road between side walls was about 11 feet, for both pedestrians and traffic. The narrowness and hump back of the bridge made it difficult and dangerous in the great coaching days. Hodgson wrote – "the Mail and Wonder coaches having each, within the last three years, once carried away the south end of its west battlements and been thrown with their passengers and horses into the river – fortunately without loss of life". So it was decided to build a new bridge, and the bailiffs and burgesses were no longer required to maintain the old bridge. This was later knocked down to be rid of the necessity of repairs or to make the new toll bridge used for all occasions. However, in 1869 a footbridge was constructed in iron using the medieval pier and abutments. It was made and erected by the firm of Swinney, which played an important part in the industry of Morpeth for 100 years. Their works were on the site now occupied by the Safeway supermarket.

In 1972, the central pier of the old bridge needed attention from the River Board. The removal of the stone arches had reduced the weight on the pier and it was being eroded. In the past bags of cement had been deposited about the stone structure. The workmen carrying out the restoration made a coffer dam of sandbags and pumped out the water. The concrete lumps and other material were removed, and I was allowed to excavate part of it.

The pier had been built on a raft or cradle of heavy oak timbers. There were pointed timbers at each end like the gables of a house and the longer timbers were crossed by half-lap timbers. All were held in position by numerous piles. One of the longer timbers was 30 feet long and about 18 inches thick. It still carried the original bark and probably dated back to the reign of Edward I. Some of these timbers were lopped and pieces can still be seen in the bed of the river. A retaining concrete wall was put about the pier and faced with stones. The timbers are under water again, which had preserved them.

When the new Telford Bridge was built in 1831 it involved the alteration of the weir, which was removed to its present position. In certain conditions of water and light the line of the old weir can be seen at an angle below the old Bridge. On the

south bank it was near the bridge abutment, but on the north bank disappears under the new bridge. A tunnel had to be constructed to carry the water to the Manorial Mill which for many years stood on the site of St George's Church. The stone-lined tunnel can be seen under the church, and the water joined the Cotting Burn at the corner of the Old Red Bull Inn. It also powered the Fulling or Wauk Mill, which was situated on the Cotting Burn at the bottom of Tommy's Field. Tommy Longstaffe was the proprietor of the building when it was converted into a public house, and named the 'Prince Albert' in 1851.

The visitor is able to descend steps from the Chantry bridge and pass under the **Telford Bridge.** The engineer was the famous Thomas Telford. John Dobson advised on the architecture – his other work can be seen at the Court House and Chantry. He was also concerned with the design of the gasworks, so that there was a lot of his work in this area. The building contractors were Thomas King and William Beldon. Thomas King did much construction in Morpeth, and King's Avenue in the northern part of the town is named after him, not royalty.

The Earl of Carlisle had a waggonway constructed from Netherton to Morpeth, some three miles down a graduated incline, so that the waggons, whether carrying coal or stone, moved by gravity and the empties were easy to pull back. Coal was provided for the Gasworks and stone for various buildings as well as the bridge. A temporary bridge of timber was thrown across the Wansbeck. This was a time of very great activity in construction and the face of the town was changing.

The Telford Bridge consists of three arches. The central one of 50 feet rises 16 feet and the side ones of 40 feet rise 13 feet. The width of the bridge is 32½ feet, and the marvel is that neither the engineer nor the constructors could have imagined the loads it takes today.

At the south end of the bridge the toll house still remains. It was constructed in such a way that the toll-keeper could look out through windows in both directions. Payment was levied on persons, vehicles and animals in order to raise money for the building and maintenance of the bridge.

What was called the **Court House and New Gaol** was built on the south side of the Wansbeck, replacing the Old Gaol in Bridge Street. In 1821 an Act for building a new prison was passed and plans for it advertised. John Dobson was successful and the building was completed under his direction in 1828. It cost £71,000 and was built to a castle plan. Dobson had spent some time studying the Welsh Castles of Edward I, and concluded that walls of a type to keep men out, could also be used to keep men in. The castle structure was much favoured at the time and in appearance it was very impressive. There was a similar building at Newcastle, since demolished, and another at Jedburgh which can still be visited as an ancient monument. It is possible that the same malefactors served their time in both Jedburgh and Morpeth Gaols. Hodgson describes Morpeth Gaol – "The gateway is an imposing building 72 feet high, and on the ground floor, has in front on the south the porter's lodge and on the north a grand stone staircase leading to the

sessions house and other apartments above: behind on the ground floor are a chapel on the right as you enter and the sick wards and bath on the left. On the second floor of the gateway is the sessions house or hall for county meetings, 92 feet by 64 and 41 feet high: it is a heptagonal semi-circle, surrounded by a gallery, large enough to hold 3-500 persons and has under it rooms for the clerk of the peace, counsel and petty jury and cells for prisoners on trial, besides a passage and lobbies for witnesses. The ceiling of this and other principal rooms are ribbed and vaulted in a style suited to the character of the exterior of the building. On the second floor and south east angle of the gateway there is also a room for the grand jury and for holding petty sessions in; and over it and the grand staircase, on the third floor, is a great hall, measuring 60 feet by 31 feet.

The governor's house contains apartments for himself and the turnkey is in the centre of the gaol and commands a view of the airing grounds and the whole suite of prisons, and is approached from the porter's lodge by a vaulted passage 104 feet long, which from its being lighted only from each end, produces a gloomy, but fine effect. The debtors' ward occupies the east, north east and south east sides of the octagon: the felons' ward is on the south and south west sides, the gateway on the west and the house of correction on the north west and north sides. The machinery for pumping the water in the house of correction side is worked by the criminals in the tread mill manner." (Hodgson)

The builders were Messrs King, Kyle and Hall and the stone came from Morpeth Quarry on the east of the town and south of the river.

The prison complex was surrounded by a wall more than 20 feet high and escapes were very few. Prisoners included striking miners, acquaintances of Thomas Burt, who later became MP for Morpeth. Miners were often strict Methodists and the gaol chaplain was surprised to be congratulated on a good sermon.

The gallows stood on Goosehill nearby, until public executions were abolished. The County Gaol continued to function until 1881, when prison accommodation was transferred to Newcastle. After this the walls were removed and sold as building stone. Goosehill Schools were built upon part of the site and the Morpeth Police retained some of the buildings. The Court House continued in use until 1980, but repairs were not carried out and there was some danger of demolition. It has been saved and is used for other purposes, both catering and residential, so that a fine building remains. It is often mistaken for "the Castle" and does in fact provide a good example of what the Gatehouse to an Edwardian castle was like with its battlements – crenellation and machicolation. Like the bridge the stonework is excellent.

While in the neighbourhood of the Telford Bridge we might cross it again to look at **St George's Church**, originally built in 1861 as English Presbyterian, but now United Reformed. Pevsner comments – "Facing the whole length of the street with its perversely stepped up W. tower ending in an octagonal spirelet".

The tower has been likened by less architecturally minded to a space-rocket. Not easily noticed is the memorial plaque to John Horsley, teacher and minister at

the former chapel in Cottingwood Lane. He was born in 1685 and educated at the Royal Grammar School, Newcastle. He took a degree at Edinburgh University and later settled in Morpeth. A scientist as well as a theologian, he was known for his pioneer work on Roman Britain, which was not published until after his death in 1731. It was a study of existing Roman remains in Britain at a time when the Roman Wall had not been used for building the Military Road. He also started collecting information for a History of Northumberland, but he died at the age of 46. His work is very highly regarded by Roman scholars. A special service was held at St George's Church in 1932, two hundred years after his death.

Looking over to the Chantry we are reminded that William Turner (1508-1566) son of a Morpeth tanner, attended the Grammar School there, and went on to Cambridge to make the acquaintance of Cranmer and Ridley, the great Reformers. However, he is now remembered for his Herbal, which has recently been reprinted as A New Herbal, edited with a modern version by George Chapman and Marilyn Tweddle. The book was very valuable as doctors depended on herbs for remedies and it was important that plants should be properly identified. His work shows that as a boy he must have spent much time botanizing along the banks of the Wansbeck and elsewhere. The boy became the "Father of English Botany". He reminds us of the birch. "I have not read of any virtue that it hath in physic. Howbeit, it served many good uses, and for none better than for seating stubborn boys, that either lie or will not learn." He also wrote – "Fishers in Northumberland pull off the outermost bark and put it in the cleft of a stick and set it in fire and hold it at the water side and make fish come together, which if they see, they strike with their leisters or salmon spears". This was a common poacher's practice. Morpeth's motto is "Inter Silvas et Flumina Habitans" – Dwelling amid woods and waters.

Opposite the Court House is **Carlisle Park**, the great attraction of Morpeth, which has helped the town to win a number of "Britain in Bloom" awards.

Old photographs show that much of the area was used for cattle grazing. In 1888 and afterwards the Countess Rosalind took over the administration of the Carlisle estates and found that Morpeth was unprofitable. Much of the land, and also town properties were sold. Lord Joicey purchased the Town Hall in 1916 and presented it to the people. The Countess presented the land which became Carlisle Park, but it took some ffme to develop, and was not officially opened until 1928, by the late Earl of Carlisle, who was then a boy of five. He was presented with a little silver mace like "Belted Will" presented to the town in 1604.

Carlisle Park is entered by ornamental iron gates, which support the coats of arms of the Earls of Carlisle and of Morpeth Borough. The lower level of the land here is laid out with lawns, pavements and beautifully flowering borders. Each year has a little garden of special design. The higher ground carries an array of larger flowers, shrubs and flowering bushes, backed by large trees. The large mound looking down into the Park is called Ha' Hill and was the original Norman Castle. It was at one time grazed, but the vegetation has been allowed to grow and now it

looks like a nature reserve, yet very attractive in its contrast to the formal gardens. It carries thorns, briars, brambles and armies of willowherb. There are paths on either side from which it can be approached, and it is worth climbing for the general view it gives of Morpeth – the old heart of the river loop, the woods and the hills beyond. The important buildings of the town can be picked out and eastwards the line of the railway. The castle which succeeded it can be viewed across the dene, with gatehouse and surrounding walls, recently repaired.

From Carlisle Park the pathway can be followed above the road and from this, near the Cenotaph, there is a rising drive into the Castle area. This can be followed and the Castle viewed from the outside. It has been repaired by the Landmark Trust for residential purposes.

The Gatehouse of Morpeth Castle, dating to the 14th century, which has been restored by the Landmark Trust for holiday accommodation.

The Castle suffered severely during the Civil War. In 1644 Scottish troops, supporting Parliament, had captured it. Then it was besieged by Scottish Royalist troops under Montrose and was beaten into surrender. Cannon fire badly damaged the walls, gatehouse and interior buildings. It was described as a "ruinous hole" and little was done to repair the damage. Interior buildings disappeared and it was not till 1846 that the Earl of Carlisle restored the gatehouse for his agent. It had appeared in prints and pictures as a romantic ruin overgrown with ivy and other vegetation. But it has excellent views, and on the way around it the town and more distant country can be surveyed. The higher path, once to the main road, can be followed to the Sun Inn, an ancient hostelry, which served thousands on the day of the

suffragette, Emily Davison's funeral in 1913. We can follow her to St Mary's, the parish church, and the oldest ecclesiastical building in the town.

St Mary's Church is approached through a lychgate on a rising path. The basement is built of stone with sloping stone seats, and an inscription on the timbers of the roof records it to have been built in 1861 in memory of A R Fenwick of Netherton. The path was lined with yew trees some of which have been removed, and the visitor is impressed by the reticulated East window with five lights. It is large and dates to the 14th century when the church was rebuilt. Looking back the Sun Inn can be seen through the lychgate. The older gravestones are near the church and there is a variety of them. Stepping back to the trees it is possible to view the whole southward aspect of the church. The chancel is tall, whereas the nave has a flat roof and the western tower has been described as "squat". The lower part of it probably dates back to the Norman period. It has diagonal buttresses and bell openingswith cusped Y tracery; Pevsner adds – "a concave-sided lead roof of pagoda type" with a fish as a weather vane.

*St. Mary's Church, Morpeth indicates that the original town was further south.
There was a Norman or earlier church, but what remains is mainly 14th century
with the Jesse window of fine stained glass.*

Though the general aspect of the building is 14th century, there is evidence of earlier structures. Dowsing has revealed that there was an early church with an apsidal east end. Then there was a larger church with extended nave and chancel and in time the north and south aisles were added. Indications are that the nave once had a pointed roof with lower outer walls. The south porch was added in the

15th century. A look at the west end of the church will show these additions in different stone, and there are blocked windows above the south aisle. On the outside also can be seen the priest's door to the chancel – medieval with medieval ironwork. Near the junction of the chancel and nave is a low side window, which was not as thought for lepers to view the services, but for the purpose of ringing the angelus bell to announce the raising of the host at mass. It could be heard in the fields and at the Catchburn Hospital and one imagines in medieval times, workers pausing to cross themselves.

Another outside feature to be noticed is the Watch house opposite the porch and at the south gate. It was constructed in 1831 to guard against body-snatchers of the time who sought to supply the medical school in Edinburgh with fresh corpses. St Mary's was conveniently on the A1 road. Adjacent to the Watch house is the Woodman monument, the Woodmans being an important family in the town. William Woodman was a town clerk, who contributed a great deal to the recording of Morpeth's history and provided Hodgson with information. The Woodman Collection in the County Record Office is very important to the study of Morpeth's history.

The north side of the chancel has two medieval gargoyles or waterspouts, no longer functional and hardly ornamental.

The original two storeyed vestry abuts on to the chancel, and the space between this and the east end of the north aisle has been filled so that there is continuous walling to the west end, where two well worn medieval effigies lie outside the tower. The entrance to the nave is through the south porch which contains a list of rectors. Hollows in the stone near the door show that knives or swords were sharpened here. The massive door retains its medieval ironwork with door knocker. The door is made of timbers both vertical and horizontal, fastened together by heavy square-headed nails. Stepping down into the church shows that the digging of numerous graves raised the level of the land outside.

Inside is the double chamfered tower arch under which is an octagonal font on four shafts. Both the north aisle and south aisle have five chamfered arches supported by octagonal piers. There are some indications that they were painted and masons' marks can also be detected. There is a recess in the wall of the south aisle, presumably to take a monument, and here the east window deserved special attention since it contains very fine medieval glass. Wilson (1870) wrote that the window was being restored by Clayton & Bell as a memorial to the wife of Benjamin Woodman. The glass depicts Christ and two saints – St Blaise and St Denis, patron saints respectively of sheep and cattle. The squint on the right side of the chancel arch, by which the priest in the chantry chapel could keep contact with the altar, has been blocked, but the corresponding one on the north side is still open.

In the last century the church had three galleries – on the west for the choir and musicians, another on the north, and the third for the school which partly obstructed the chancel arch. These were removed in the time of Reverend Francis Grey, but unfortunately the rood screen was damaged and also removed. The seating was

altered, so that the church was much more open. Another oak screen was erected in memory of members of the Brumell family.

From this screen one may gaze at the glory of the church – the Jesse window at the east end, filled with coloured glass, much of it medieval. It was repaired by Wailes, the Gateshead glass expert, in memory of John Bolland, one time curate of Morpeth. It depicts Jesse's dream. The family tree of David, descending to the Virgin Mary, to whom the church was dedicated and Jesus. The panels of the window include 16 prophets, who foretold the birth of Christ, the Saviour. The window is specially beautiful when the eastern sun shines through the glass and one can imagine the glory of the church, when there was much more medieval painted glass in the windows.

In the south wall of the chancel below the window are three stepped sedilia or seats for the priests. They are more elaborate than usual and decorated. Two carved heads are thought to be likenesses of Edward III and his wife, Queen Philippa, as at Blanchland. On the other side of the chancel are the vestry door and the door of an ambry or cupboard, both with original medieval ironwork.

I will not speculate about the quatrefoil opening from the sacristy into the church, there has been too much speculation already!

The churchyard is worth exploring. The gravestones are mementoes of Morpeth's history. The original church yard has been extended several times, especially in the time of Rev Francis Grey. He was responsible for improved layout and the planting of trees, notably limes and Wellingtonias, which rise to a great height. They are a contrast to the old yew trees that may have been in place since medieval times, when they were grown for making bow staves – archery was compulsory in Henry VIII's time as a sport for schools. Football was forbidden. Yew trees are usually much older than supposed according to experts; 1,000 years not being uncommon. Yews which are poisonous were grown in churchyards to keep cattle out and Morpeth cattle grazed on the nearby common. The growth of trees has tended to hide the church and larger trees overshadow it. In 1850 this was not so and when in 1856, a memorial was erected like a Gothic spire to Reverend John Bolland, Curate of Morpeth, it would be the most outstanding feature of the town, standing on the hill above the church – more than 33 feet high in shining stone. The curate had died in the Holy Land on a pilgrimage at the age of thirty three and was buried on Mount Sion. Besides this monument, there was in his memory the stained glass in the church and Bolland School on Pottery Bank.

By contrast Reverend Francis Grey and his wife, formerly Lady Elizabeth Howard, repose under flat gravestones of medieval style, beneath the shadow of Bolland's spire and overgrown with brambles. Above, the monument to Emily Davison, who died in 1913, has been refurbished.

Monuments tend to extend westwards where the limit is a wall and another watch house. In the area nearest the wall are the tombstones of men – mostly

Polish – who fell in the last war. There is a rather derelict area, lacking monuments, where inmates of the workhouse were buried and some from the hospital.

The extended graveyard had a closure order in 1988, and only relatives of persons in existing graves, where there is still space, can be buried here. The present extension is strictly a cemetery under the control of the Council and not of the Church. Here all denominations may be interred. The burial place is an important piece of social history. Morpeth churchyard is adjacent to the golf course, which is upon land that was the common, shared by freeholders. There can be seen the old medieval plough riggs, that marked the separate strips. They still provide difficulties for the golfers, and there are prehistoric earthworks, only visible from aerial photographs. The Wanney Railway formerly cut across the common which stretches to the High House road and provides an attractive walk. Horse races are still held on the common after the Beating of the Bounds on St Mark's Day. There is also a sports area, but the grandstand has been converted into housing. During the War there was an army camp here, which was used for Polish resettlement. There was also a Polish Military Hospital and a number of Polish soldiers and airmen have settled in Morpeth.

Along the Newcastle Road are the Cottage Hospital, the Headquarters of Castle Morpeth Borough Council and County Hall, but we make our way back to the town centre, passing Rectory park for which the Old Rectory was demolished. A fine Georgian building was constructed in the 18th century and extended by Rev Ekins and Rector Francis Grey, who needed additional accommodation. There were several acres of land, hence the present housing estate. The Church Burn can be seen in its deep gully, before it is piped underground. Deuchar park was a deep valley, which was used as a refuse tip and then grassed over. Shrubs and trees were planted, making the area pleasantly attractive amid the noise of road and rail. A large boulder commemorates Farquhar Deuchar who gave the land. His grave and another memorial are in St Mary's churchyard.

On the other side of the road the Church Burn re-appears for a time at great depth and beyond is the new Allery Banks housing estate.

THE RAILWAY

The railway has recently been electrified and the new trains pass almost silently. The main London to Edinburgh line here makes a sharp bend, which taken too quickly, has caused several serious accidents, especially in 1969 and 1984. In 1969 the Aberdonian, travelling at 80 mph on a bend with a 40 mph limit was derailed and broke in half. Six persons were killed and 121 injured (three dying later) and the north platform awning was damaged. In 1984 the Aberdeen to London express travelling at 88 mph on a 50 mph speed limit, crashed into houses on the embankment. Passengers were injured, but no deaths. Safety devices have been fitted on both lines as a warning of too high speed. The station can be reached by the main road, turning under the bridge or by a side path and a subway. At the top of the steps from the subway there is a fine tiled map, which shows the extent of railway

track in the NE region in the first decade of this century. It is very interesting to compare with the present situation. Then all trains (except Tyneside Electric) were powered by steam, using enormous quantities of coal. There were multiple branch lines and colliery lines with coal depots at stations. Morpeth Station was the meeting place of several branches.

The first train of the NE Railway reached Morpeth on 1 March 1847. In time connections were established with Berwick and Edinburgh, involving the building of massive viaducts. In 1857 the Blyth and Tyne Railway arrived, linking Morpeth to Bedlington, Ashington, Newsham, Seaton Delaval and Newcastle. The Company had its own terminus at Morpeth at what are now called the Old Station Buildings which still stand opposite the station.

In 1862 the Wansbeck Valley Line was being developed and it used the Blyth and Tyne Station. The track crossed the road by bridge south of the present bridge and another bridge took it over the road, near the Cottage Hospital. It crossed the common towards Meldon, Angerton, Middleton, Scots Gap, Knowesgate, Ray, West Woodburn and Redesmouth, linking with the North British line to the Border. In 1870 another link was established with a line from Scots Gap Junction to Rothbury. Country areas benefitted from the better communications and heavy loads – coal, stone, timber, lime, ironware and military supplies – could be conveyed quickly and comparatively cheaply. Morpeth became busy with rail traffic, and the mail coaches and other long distance vehicles were no longer needed. There was still much business for horse traffic in local delivery. All sorts of commodities travelled by rail.

There is a lot of good railway architecture in both bridges and station buildings. Morpeth Station is a fine building, designed by Benjamin Green, who was also responsible for the Theatre Royal and Grey's Monument in Newcastle. Two lions, recently acquired from Tynemouth, guard the station entrance.

In 1874 the NE Railway took over the Blyth and Tyne and new curves were constructed to link the two lines. A link had also been established with the Wanney line, so that the bridge over the main line was not needed. The buildings of the Blyth and Tyne were used for goods traffic and storage. A walk along Coopie's Lane by the railway, shows something of the railway's history. A new higher footbridge has been constructed for pedestrians to cross to the north of the line and further eastwards is the level crossing. The old footbridge was used by generations of train spotters, and the new bridge provides a grand stand view.

Looking southwards, there stretches the industrial estate with the railway sidings and stores. Beyond was the Morpeth Cattle Mart which was closed in 1985 and houses have been built on the site. Looking westwards the eye follows the shining metals to the Ha' Hill and the Court House. The churches, the Clock Tower and Town Hall can be picked out. St George's Hospital situated on Cottingwood has lost its tall brick chimney and beyond rises the mound of the Butterwell opencast site. It is not always realised how close Morpeth was to coal and numerous old bell pits can be detected. Further eastwards Pegswood can be seen and the line of

the railway coming over the viaduct and past Park House. It is a very pleasant walk to continue to the entrance of this farm and across the fields by a farm lane to another bridge over the railway for extensive prospects.

We continue down the line of what was the old waggonway, past Salisbury Street, Kensington Cottages and Gladstone Street to the River, where the waggonway passed on wooden staithes towards the Gasworks, which have been demolished.

The iron bridge across the river was transferred from Oldgate in 1936. There is a ford below it, which is used for vehicles, and the river hereabouts is very attractive. In 1738 a plan was made of the River Wansbeck from the sea to Morpeth in consideration of the possible development of a canal. The fifth and final lock would have been at East Mill, but the scheme was never attempted and Morpeth had to rely on the waggonway and horse traffic. There is an attractive walk from the iron bridge along the south bank of the river to the centre of the town.

Crawford Cottages on the north bank were constructed for employees of the Morpeth Gas Company. The gasometers disappeared long ago, but the retort house and stone buildings stood till quite recently, used as a Council Depot. The stonework and structure were of good quality, blending with the Bridge and Court House. Comfort House has been built upon the site, a large building with patterned brickwork and river views. The river walk overlooks the flood protection wall and follows the streets called Bennett's Walk and Melbourne Terrace, where are some old stone structures and houses with mixed materials.

On the other side of the river appear twin mansions dating back to the middle of the last century. They were Beechfield House, built for NI Wright, timber merchant and the Willows for G Brumell, solicitor. The owners were friends and the similar properties had cottages, stables and extensive gardens. The houses were built in brick with stone quoins and are now the premises of the County Library. They provide excellent services, so that Northumberland has one of the highest book issues per head of population in the country. The adjacent car park was once the Terrace Park with flower beds, walks, trees and views of the river. A few iron railings are a reminder of this, and there were stepping stones across the river. From the south side we get a most attractive view of the bridges and St George's Church, which replaced the manorial mill. In recent years an upper floor has been inserted with dormer windows looking to the river. It was built in 1860 and the west tower with a spire, shows that Non-Conformity was asserting its presence. The architect was Mr Thompson.

The pathway we are following passes under the south arch of Telford's bridge, by which water only passes in time of flood. The remains of the medieval bridge can be viewed before climbing steps to reach it and returning to the Chantry.

Bridge Street extends from the bridge to the Town Hall and is regarded as the main street for shops. The buildings were mostly residential, in that craftsmen and traders lived above their shops, but now they are altered to shopping and storage

only. This involves new street fronts at ground level and the removal of partitions within the buildings. However, above the shop window level, some interesting architecture can be noticed. A number of houses date back to the 18th century or earlier, and it was usual for them to have cellars and wells. Many of these have been filled in. The newsagent's opposite the Chantry with mock Tudor "black and white" of 1936, has exposed beams, rough hewn with the adze, crooked and knotted. Jenning's premises opposite show something of the old splendour at the higher level, but the pride of Bridge Street must be the Black Bull, which is also a reminder of the cattle market. A 1780 handbill informs that it had stabling for 80 horses, and the upper room facing the street has a fine 17th century plaster ceiling. Pevsner says – "Of the houses only the Black Bull needs mention with a nice Adamish doorway and a bow window projecting pleasantly into the street". It was important as a coaching inn till the advent of the railway. On the other side of the street is the Old Gaol, which has retained its street front after extensive renovation. It was a warren of buildings, including Lord Dacre's tower. After use as a prison, it became the site of a brewery with complicated cellars. Now the premises are used by the Department of Social Security.

The Morpeth Herald shop also deserves notice since it retains the old front, with a step up from the dirty streets and the two stage door when top and bottom opened separately. The paper started in 1854 and remained in the hands of the Mackay family until 1983. The Queen's Head, faced in modern mock Tudor, is an ancient hostelry, and still contains a 17th century Pye fireplace. In 1772 John Scott, later Lord Eldon, stayed here with his bride, Bessie Surtees, after their Scottish elopement.

Then we reach the **Town Hall,** which overlooks the market square and is still used for official and public meetings. It was designed in 1714 for the Earl of Carlisle by Vanbrugh and restored by J R Johnson in 1869-70 after damage by fire. Pevsner describes it – "A fine broadly designed five bay front, with arched three bay ground floor, lying a little back between the two towers. The front is band-rusticated, the towers are faced with smooth ashlar".

It was presented to the Town by Lord Joicey, who purchased it from the Earl of Carlisle in 1917. The plaque commemorating this generous gift is dated 1919. The lower part of the Town Hall was used for market purposes. It is still a place for fairs, fetes and gatherings. The impressive staircase is a good reminder of the Vanburgh style and has portraits of Morpeth men of importance on the walls. The stairs lead into the attractive wooden panelled ballroom, and along the landing to the Mayor's Parlour and the Council Chamber. In both places interesting items of Morpeth's history are kept. In the Mayor's Parlour are the silverware, pictures, books and portraits. In the Council Chamber are four of the guild boxes and the town hutch with its seven locks. There is a rope used for bull baiting, the branks or bridle for a scold, halberds used by outriders, cannon balls fired at the Castle, but most important the mace donated to the borough by Lord William Howard in 1604. There is a portrait of Earl Grey of the Reform Bill, father of Rev Francis Grey, Rector of Morpeth, and by contrast another of Tommy Longstaffe, an old-style

innkeeper. His inn was the Prince Albert, converted from the old fulling mill on the Cottingburn, near the junction with the Wansbeck. He also kept a menagerie and his field, called Tommy's Field, is used for allotments. Another important Morpethian was John Rastrick, who invented a threshing machine. His son became a famous railway engineer; their house was on Newgate Street.

Adjacent to the Town Hall at the junction of Oldgate and the New Market is the **Clock Tower.** Pevsner and others have written of it as "medieval" and it is built of Medieval stone, which came from Newminster. It was not on the 1604 map and may have been moved from the other end of Oldgate. It contains six bells which were given to the borough by Major General Edmond Main in 1705. The bells were intended for Berwick, which did not elect him. Morpeth made him a Member of Parliament and was rewarded with the bells. It can now be said that bells of Berwick can be heard in Morpeth, even the curfew.

The Tower was restored in 1760 and the clock is said to have come from Bothal Castle. Like Wallington's clock it only had one pointer and so the spaces between each number were four to denote the quarters of the hours. The tower has been somewhat daunted by the higher YMCA buildings of 1905. The bells have tolled and chimed through the ages, calling to meetings and to the church, lamenting the dead and rejoicing in celebrations and victories. The tower was used as a lockup for offenders and for a time the fish market stood in front of it. Now in front of it on the site of the Market Cross is the Hollon Fountain re-erected 1885.

Mary Trotter came to live with her uncle Dr William Trotter at "Bon Accord" in Newgate Street. She learnt to love Morpeth and in 1855 married Richard Hollon of York, where she went to live. She provided the clock for St George's Church in 1861. Later she bequeathed a fund to provide annuities of £10 a year for 13 old women and 12 old men, with extra coal and meat at Christmas. In gratitude Morpeth town provided a memorial fountain, which benefitted both man and beast. "Blessed is he that considereth the poor."

In **Oldgate** St Bede's Place housed a Catholic Church before the building of St Robert's Church on the other side of the street (1850). The architect was T Gibson of Newcastle and the style is described as Early English. It has a nave, chancel and a well proportioned tower at the west end, surmounted by an octagonal spire, rising to a height of 119 feet. It has a rood screen and colourful glass in the windows. St Robert was the first abbot of Newminster.

Collingwood House, an adjacent building is used by the Church. It was the home of Admiral Lord Collingwood, who was second in command to Nelson at the Battle of Trafalgar (1805), taking over when Nelson was killed. He was unable to spend much time at Morpeth because of his naval service and died at sea in 1810. There is a monument to him at Tynemouth with guns from his ship, the Royal Sovereign. Collingwood House is an attractive Georgian building in red brick. The gardens stretched along the river, and Collingwood called them his quarter deck. St Robert's Catholic Church was built on this land in 1850 and a school was also built. This has recently been replaced by brick buildings of traditional design.

On the other side of Oldgate were Matheson's Gardens, once a great attraction with flowers, trees and fruit. Oldgate Court, an award winning housing development, has covered the area, but a number of trees have been retained. In fact it could be regarded as a series of interlinked courts, fringing the river. Here again attractive brickwork has been used.

Pevsner, who omitted a number of good buildings, thought that Oldgate ended harshly. There was, until 1970, a narrow girder bridge over the river and a ford. This has been replaced by a fine curved modern structure, which fits in beautifully, and from it the length of Oldgate can be observed to the Clock Tower.

The visitor is able to walk back along the river eastwards to the New Market and the Riverside Leisure Centre. The New Market was the site of the Cattle Market until it was transferred to Stobhill. The town market with stalls is held here on Wednesdays, though at present there is a dispute limiting its use. On the other side of the river is the promenade opened in 1936. This stretch of the river is also used for boating. Westwards from the bridge are the High Stanners. These were stony areas caused by the upcast of the river. However, this was embanked and the ground levelled with grass and trees planted. The river fronts of the houses of Newgate Street with their stepped gardens appear beautifully over the river. Forty eight stepping stones called Bakehouse steps provide a quick way over the Wansbeck to Newgate Street. The tree-lined walk continues to the Skinnery Bridge erected in 1904, which can be crossed to Dogger Bank, the ascent of which leads to Newgate Street.

In **Newgate Street** the square is called Buller's Green, which was once a separate township and has an assorted collection of houses. One house at North Place has a plaque to Dr Morrison, the missionary to China, who once lived at Morpeth. He was born in 1782 and died in Canton in 1834. House No 19 near this is constructed roughly from Newminster stone and timber. It may well date back to the 16th century.

On the other side of Newgate Street is Bow Villa, built in 1824 in Dobson Style. It still has some 'blind' windows that existed in window tax time. The big house on Pottery Bank, Hillbrow, built in Tudor style, belonged to R Oliver of Oliver's Mill. It was used by the County Council as a children's home and assessment centre, but is now vacant. A small alley called Beggar's lane, runs down between the houses to the Cottingburn and Cottingwood Lane. It dips down past long gardens and over a little bridge to the entrance of King Edward VI School. A sluice gate shows that the waters of the burn were controlled for industrial purposes, since the tanneries were near.

The upper part of Newgate Street appears as Silver Street on the old maps and was graced by a number of fine houses, some of which remain. One is Beeswing, named after a famous racehorse belonging to William Ord of Nunnykirk. Between 1835 and 1842 the mare won 51 of 64 races, and stayed here on her way to retirement and mothering further winners at Nunnykirk.

Opposite is Dawson Place, built in 1974 on the site of some derelict buildings and the former tanneries. Built in attractive brick and in a garden setting on both

sides of the Cottingburn, it has won architectural awards. Adjacent are a number of fine 18th century houses, used first as residences then as the Girls High School and Teachers Centre. Wansbeck House with a castellated gateway was once the home of Joseph Crawhall, a famous artist. Bon Accord was the house of Dr William Trotter, uncle of Mary Hollon. Both Lansdowne House (No 90) and Dunedin House are fine examples of 18th century housing. The Black and Grey Horses Inn has provided its services for some 200 years. This stands on the entrance to Copper Chare and the building on the other side was the old Morpeth CWS premises.

Below this is attractive arcading, constructed to separate the entrance to St James's Church from the street and to be a memorial to Rev Francis Grey, Rector, who was responsible for the building of the church in this place and in the Norman style of architecture. The screen was erected in 1890, recording that the Rector had served 48 years in the parish. With his ability and family connections he could have gone elsewhere, but devoted his life to Morpeth. The inscription above the arches reads "Lord I have loved the habitation of Thy house and the place where Thine Honour dwelleth".

The arcading is in the style of Newminster and the pillars are of Frosterley marble, black in colour but with many fossils. The west door of the church is approached down an avenue of lime trees. The architect was Benjamin Ferry and the design was inspired by the Norman Cathedral of Monreale in Sicily, a country like England conquered by the Normans. The exterior gives a very good idea of the Norman style – strong with round headed windows and doors. It consists of nave

St. James's Church, Morpeth, built 1843-6 to the designs of Benjamin Ferry in Norman style, from Monreale in Sicily.

with aisles and transepts and a central tower. The chancel has an apsidal east end. The stonework is excellent and the exterior comparatively plain. The interior is attractively decorative. In the nave the arches are supported by 12 quatrefoil columns, said to represent the 12 apostles; 11 are decorated and one called the Judas column is not; it is also called the "apprentice piece". The coloured glass of the windows is by Wailes of Gateshead. The wall painting or frescoes in the east end, illustrating the Betrayal, Crucifixion and Resurrection of Christ, were designed by Clayton and Bell. Saints and prophets are also depicted. The main part of the building was completed in 1846, the tower with spire in 1852; and in 1881 the choir vestry was built, relieving the south aisle.

After nearly a century and a half of existence, the Church presents problems of maintenance and repair. This church took the place of the Chantry and a new school was designed by Benjamin Ferrey on the Cottingwood site. For no good reason this was demolished when another school was built. On this same lane was Horsley's school and chapel, built about 1720. It has since served many purposes, but was lately converted into a house named Kirkville.

At the east end of St James's is the Rotary Garden, where St Thomas's Well was situated. Overlooking it is the present Methodist Church. There were two Methodist Churches in Manchester Street. The Primitive Methodist Church has become St James's Market and the Wesleyan Methodist Church, built in 1884 in Gothic style, now houses the Boys Brigade.

From Manchester Street Well Way leads to the Safeway Supermarket, built on Swinney's site and the Back Riggs Shopping Centre together with the Bus Station.

Back in Newgate Street some good 18th century houses have been converted entirely to shops. Sim and Webb (Chemists) and Stokers (Butchers) retain the older shop fronts. The Conservative Club occupies Harle House, which in the early 19th century was the Headmaster's house. The Grammar School stayed here from a time in transit from the Chantry to Cottingwood. In the cellars of Robson House are, now hidden, the ovens of the bakehouse, hence Bakehouse Yard and Bakehouse steps over the river.

In 1689 a severe fire broke out in Morpeth and some 50 houses were destroyed. There is evidence of the reconstruction in the lower part of Newgate Street, where a number of buildings have characteristic Dutch gables, as the one next to the present Joe's Fruit Shop. The Wheatsheaf building was demolished where Barnado's shop has been built, but Wheatsheaf Yard shows what the old courtyards were like.

We have to leave the Market Place and follow the river eastwards, where we run into industry, both quarrying and coal mining. In the fields there are hollows or holes that were bell pits and the stone quarries are obviously extensive.

East Mill was on the same site in 1604 and a timber beam gives the date 1798, and in 1892 further construction took place. In its time this mill has been powered by water, steam and electricity. The buildings included house, stables and outhouses. Since the mill ceased to work it has been used for various industrial purposes and the weir is still maintained.

East Mill, Morpeth. Originally powered by water, later by steam and then by electricity from steam.

Bothal viaduct carrying the Newcastle to Edinburgh railway over the Wansbeck. It was completed in 1849 by Robert Stephenson and has nine arches.

Next to the mill is Swinney's Sports ground, and a by-way leads to a Bailey bridge over the river to Quarry Woods, where there are pleasant walks along to the railway viaduct. On the other side of the main road on the Holburn (or How Burn) can be seen the relics of coal mining – holes and spoil heaps. At the top of Whorral Bank are the remains of Morpeth Moor Colliery and the Butterwell opencast excavations. There are other old sites of coal working on the way to Pegwood (or Pegswurth as it was called), which is essentially a colliery village, while Bothal remains an estate village. By a curious division of local authority boundaries, Pegswood is in Castle Morpeth, while Bothal comes under Wansbeck. The main railway line to Scotland passes between the villages. Pegswood Colliery has been demolished and the pit heap converted into a Country Park from which there are varied views.

To the north is **Longhirst Hall,** built in 1824 to the designs of John Dobson for Mr Lawson. It later became Joicey property, the family having made their fortune in coal mining. The hall has recently been transformed into a business college, which provides management training and conference facilities. It has most impressive Corinthian columns to the Western entrance portico. The setting is beautiful woodland, through which the burn passes on its way to join the Wansbeck. Bothal can be reached from Morpeth by a pleasant and interesting footpath through the woods. There are also footpaths from Pegswood to this delightful village, which deserves special attention.

Longhirst Hall, built in 1824 to the designs of John Dobson, and now being developed as an educational and business centre.

CHAPTER VII: BOTHAL VILLAGE, CHURCH AND CASTLE

"The village is in every respect worthy of the beautiful surroundings and forms a sweet picture of rural peace and contentment. The cottages are prettily and substantially built with tastefully planted flower gardens in front. With its substantial cottages clustered in a steep wooded hollow where the wooded Wansbeck winds round in loveliness, it is one of the most attractive villages in Northumberland". (Tomlinson)

The picture is still the same today. Hodgson wrote in 1830 summing up the rest of the river – "Poet or painter has never yet done justice to the ever varying charms of the course of this lovely stream from her foundations in the wild moors about the Wanney Crags, till in the lone sequestered woods of Bothal and Sheepwash, she begins to put on her beautiful and bridal robes before she weds with the ocean".

Much has since changed here. Sheepwash was the tidal limit of the river and by this time Ashington (Essendun), the vale of ashes, was losing its ash trees to fire and quarrying. The railway missed Bothal, and a straight road from Pegswood to Ashington has removed the hazards of Bothal Bank. Mining villages grew at Pegswood and Ashington on the Portland estate. Bothal appears to be a quiet and secluded village, but it has seen a great deal of activity. How many times did the Scots make their raids and how extensive were the repairs that had to be made to village, church and castle?

Bothal, meaning Bota's Hall, takes its name from Anglo Saxon times. If the interpretation is as Bothel in Cumbria, it still means a dwelling or house and shows that here was an early settlement, to which a wooden church was added with the coming of Christianity. Over four or five centuries before the Normans came, there could have been several churches and halls of which there are no visible remains today.

The names of places around Bothal indicate that it was a heavily wooded area – Hirst and Longhirst, Stobswood, Woodhorn and Ashington. There were a number of parks at Morpeth, Widdrington and Bothal – oak trees were plentiful and used for building purposes.

In Norman times Bothal was granted by the King to Guy de Balliol, Baron of Bywell. The Balliols were a powerful family with lands on both sides of the Border. William Bertram married Guy's daughter Alice and was granted the lesser barony of Bothal. It was held by military service to the king of three knights, when he needed them. The Bertrams also held Mitford and founded Brinkburn Priory, besides making endowments to Newminster and Tynemouth.

A hall or castle was constructed on the site of the present castle. Hugh of Morwick did military service. Juliana, widow of Walter, held 24 acres of land for the annual payment of one pound of pepper. Five tenants paid this one pound of

pepper, which seems strange till we realise how valuable it was in those days. A large proportion of cattle, sheep and pigs had to be killed in autumn, since there was not the fodder to see them through the winter. The carcasses were preserved in salt from the local salt pans, evaporated from the brine. Pepper was desired by the more wealthy to cover the taste of salty and perhaps decaying meat. The peasants had to manage with salty meat and herbs. Fish was compulsory on Fridays and every day for the religious. Fish and eels could be obtained from the river and sea, being kept for a time in fish ponds. Hunting the deer was the privilege of the King and the barons. Dire penalties were inflicted on others. The right of "free warren" was granted by the King and rabbits were kept in special areas. Coneygarth near Bothal is a reminder. Rabbits were not prolific and had to be preserved from common poaching.

There may have been a stone church in pre-Norman times, but there was certainly a stone church with an apsidal east end in the early Norman period. There was also an early church at Sheepwash, connected with the bridge and hospital there. The buildings have disappeared, but there has been evidence of a graveyard, and the font, once used for farm purposes, is now in Bothal churchyard. Westwards of Bothal in the Wansbeck valley was the little Lady Chapel with its attendant holy man or hermit.

We learn that Robert Pinzun of Peggesworth (Pegswood) held 12 acres by the payment of two geese on the day of St Michael. In 1294 a survey by Edward I showed that Robert Bertram had the right to take felons and hang them on his gallows. He had the assize of bread and ale – the right to supervise both quality and quantity. In his demesne lands of Bothal and Hebburn, he had the right of free warren. His son, Sir Roger Bertram, attended Edward's Parliament as a knight of the shire. The Bertrams were involved in the Scottish Wars. Another Sir Robert Bertram in 1343 was granted by Edward III a licence to crenellate his manor house at Bothal – that is to construct a fully defensive castle. The Royal Arms have pride of place among the shields that decorate the gatehouse.

Sir Robert Bertram fought valiantly at the Battle of Neville's Cross (1346) when the Scots were decisively defeated. The King was waging war in France (Crecy), but awarded Sir Robert £200 for the capture of William Douglas in battle. His daughter Helen, married Robert de Ogle, by which union the Ogles became Lords of Bothal. Sir Robert, son of Helen, had lost his father at an early age and his mother married again. She and her third husband, David Holgrave, established a chantry in Bothal Church for the purpose of saying prayers for the dead. Robert, Helen's son, was Lord of Ogle. He took part in Border battles and was present at Otterburn in 1388. He died in 1410 and was buried in Hexham Abbey. On his death it had been arranged that Sir John Bertram should take over Bothal and his brother Sir Robert Ogle would be Baron of Ogle. However, he was not content with this, and Robert besieged his brother in Bothal Castle. He came "with 200 men at arms and archers, partly soldiers and partly Scotchmen, all enemies of the King and in a warlike manner invested the castle of Bothal with escapes, parvises, hurdises and other ordnance of war and after besieging it for four days got possession of it by forcible entry". (Hodgson)

Eventually Sir John was legally restored to his inheritance by the King. Sir Robert continued his military activities, playing a prominent part in the Border Wars. In 1418 he owned six castles and towers. He became Member of Parliament and Sheriff. He it was who recaptured the castle of Wark-on-Tweed by making use of the drainage tunnel and surprising the Scots within. At times he was Constable of Norham and Warden of Roxburgh Castle, which belonged to the English King. He died in 1436, having extended his properties as the Ogle family were doing. Sir John at Bothal had adopted the name of Bertram and he too was prominent in Border affairs. During the latter part of the 14th century when the castle was standing high and new built, the church was being restored and extended as a burial place for Bertrams and Ogles. The Ogles were involved in the Wars of the Roses, and supported the House of York.

Ralph, third Lord Ogle, was involved in Scottish campaigns of 1494 and 1496. He escorted Princess Margaret in 1503 on her way to marry James IV of Scotland. He died in 1513, and his alabastor tomb is in the south aisle of Bothal Church. His son Robert fought at the Battle of Flodden (1513), and was knighted on the field of battle by the Earl of Surrey. He met the exiled Queen of Scotland at Morpeth in 1515, and was involved in Border warfare. For a time he was Captain of Norham Castle, and in 1519 received a royal award for casting down Scottish castles, including Cessford. There were many Ogles in his force, including Cuthbert Ogle, parson of Ford. Robert died in 1532 and was succeeded by his son Robert, 5th Lord Ogle. He was able to serve the King with 100 horsemen. In 1536 he was appointed Vice Warden of the Marches. He was engaged in the Scottish Wars that led to the Battle of Solway Moss (1542), and was later killed in a skirmish. Cuthbert Ogle, parson of Ford was taken prisoner. Lord Ogle was buried as requested in his will, in Bothal Church. His son Robert became 6th Lord Ogle and served as Deputy Warden and MP in Edward VI's reign. In 1554 Thomas Ogle, a cleric, was presented to the livings of both Bothal and Sheepwash which were combined for the first time.

In 1562 the 6th Lord was buried in Bothal Church "without pomp" beside his parents, and was succeeded by his half brother Cuthbert. He was a Member Parliament and helped defeat the rebels of 1569, the Rebellion of the North. He commissioned a survey of his manor of Bothal in 1576 which indicates that it was well administered and the lord was quite wealthy.

Improvements were made to castle and church. Lord Cuthbert was proud of his family tree and a pedigree was made out for him. It was placed in red letters on the south side wall of the chancel of Bothal Church. The Ogles had great pride in their name as is shown 20 July 1583 in the will of Philip Grene of Morpeth – "I do humbly crave them that they (Francis Dacre & Nicholas Ridley) will see my said wiffe & children mayntained in law, for reformation of this cruel murder, committed on me by George Ogle, John Ogle, sons of James Ogle of Causey Park, Patrick & Martyne Ogle of Tritlington, Alexander Ogle, Anthony Milbourn with others, whom I fully charge with my death, hawen no cause against me but I compared the Dacres' bloude to be as good as Ogles." Dacres were Lords of Morpeth and intermarried with the Howards, another noble family.

Lord Cuthbert Ogle had no son and got a licence to alienate his property to his daughter Jane, who in 1583 married Edward, second son of the Earl of Shrewsbury. Lord Cutherbert Ogle died on 20 November 1597 at Cockle Park, another of his towers, and was buried in Bothal Church, the end of a particular piece of pedigree. Edward Talbot, who became Earl of Shrewsbury, lived at Bothal and died there 23 February 1618. He was buried, as his wife was later, at Westminster.

Jane's sister, who became Baroness Ogle, married in 1591 Sir Charles Cavendish of Welbeck, so that both sisters were related to Bess of Hardwick, whose four husbands included a Cavendish and an Earl of Shrewsbury.

Catherine, Baroness Ogle, died at Bothal, but like her husband was buried at Bolsover. Their son, William, born in 1593 became Earl of Newcastle, Baron of Ogle and Bothal, attendant on Charles Prince of Wales, and in the Civil War was Commander of the royalist forces of Charles I in the North, till defeated at Marston Moor in 1644. He went into exile and occupied himself with a riding school. He compiled a classic work on horsemanship, but his finances suffered severely from the sequestration of his estates. After the Restoration in 1660, he recovered his estates and Ogle Castle was rebuilt, depicted as a moated mansion with four corner towers standing high. The Duke's son lived here until his father's death when he moved to Welbeck. His son married the heiress, Elizabeth Percy, but he died and the Percy estates went to the Duke of Somerset (1682) by marriage. The Percy and Newcastle estates would have been a huge combine. The Newcastle heiress married John Holles who became Duke of Newcastle. Their daughter Lady Henrietta Cavendish Holles married in 1713 Edward Harley, Earl of Oxford, and is said to have brought him £500,000.

George Mark, acting as an assistant to Horsley and quoted in Hodgson, gives a description of Bothal at this time. The village is "situated very low and dignified with the remains of a stately old castle, anciently the estate of the Ogles and now the possession of the Earl of Oxford. The church is well built and situated just before the castle gates. There is a free school, lately erected by the charitable contributions of the present vicar, Mr Stafford. The village stands immediately on the north banks of the river Wansbeck, which is joined at that place by a small rivulet called Bothal Burn, which runs nearly round the village, and discharges itself into the river on the east side of the church. The soil near the village is accounted very good. There is an abundance of coal and freestone, but no limestone but what is brought from Sunderland by the sea. The village has round it a great deal of wood and planting and the river between this and Morpeth has the most rural appearance that can be. The village is well watered and has a well on the bankhead, accounted the finest water in the county and that formerly was conveyed by pipes to the castle." (Hodgson) Buck, the artist, depicted the Castle at this time (1728).

The Earl of Oxford was a great collector of books – the Harleian Collection was acquired by the British Museum. His daughter, Margaret married in 1734 William Bentinck, 2nd Duke of Portland. Since that time successive Dukes of

Portland have owned the Bothal estates. The 3rd Duke married Lady Dorothy, daughter of the Duke of Devonshire and added the name of Cavendish to his own. Welbeck Abbey was the usual residence of the Dukes of Portland.

We have a description of Bothal given by Hodgson (1832) – "Besides the church and the castle, the present village of Bothal consists of a few cottages having chimney tops of wickerwork, a school house, ale house and certain farm premises." White in 1847 wrote – "This village is very much improved within the last few years, the houses have been nearly all rebuilt".

He gave the population of Bothal demesne as 244 people. Elizabeth Bootyman kept the Castle Inn and George Cooper was the blacksmith. Thomas Coxon was woodman and gardener. George Gallon combined the job of joiner with the duties of parish clerk. Wm Sample was the agent of the Duke of Portland. Robert Spearman was the corn miller and Thomas Townsend, the school teacher. The Rector was Reverend H Hopwood MA whose rectory was over the fields at Sheepwash. He was assisted by a curate, Edward Lacey, and made some improvements to the church. Hodgson had described the church as needing some attention. There were several steps down to the church, since the soil upcast from grave digging had heightened the level of the ground south of the church. The north door in the nave had been closed, probably on account of heating. The north-west corner of the church had been converted to a hypocaust or furnace room "which does not answer the purpose for which it was built". The east window of the chancel was similar to the eastern windows of the north and south aisles. The tracery of the windows was "bespangled with devices in coloured glass and the walls are hung with lozenge-shaped panels of wood, bearing texts of scripture". The genealogy of the lords of Ogle "had been long painted in black letters on the south wall of the chancel and was lately retouched and renewed". (Hodgson)

He included a print of the church, which showed stone waterspouts thrusting out from the roofs of both nave and chancel. The chancel had a low roof and the gable above the chancel arch stood solitary and unattached.

Dr John Sharpe, on his visitation in 1826 "had a few words to give, but I begged them to look at their spouts and restore the old heraldic blazonry on the timbers of the roof and to repair the folios (of the library). The monument of the Bertrams, that of Ann Wilson, the Ogle pedigree on the wall, the painted glass in the windows and the carved capitals on the north side of the entrance into the chancel are all curious and should be preserved." He added – "They have three bells, two of them not being in the best order." (Hodgson) Hebburn was a chapelry of Bothal and the chapel itself deteriorated. In 1793 it was rebuilt, the proprietors of lands in the parish paying for the nave, and Rev Smalridge, rector of Bothal paid for the chancel. There is a large square monument to members of the Smalridge family – the only one that is seen north of the church in Hodgson's print.

In 1870 F R Wilson, an architect, completed a survey of the churches of the Archdeaconry of Lindisfarne, with plans and views of 75 churches. After describing the church of Bothal, he continued – "The aspect of this church is exceedingly

venerable, reverend and devotional. But the conditions of it is not good and scarcely safe. Both the arcades are much out of the perpendicular; and things generally look awry and ready to give way. There is a descent of five steps from the doorway to the floor of the church on the south side, where the soil has accumulated to such an extent, that it nearly reaches the sills of the windows. On the north side, owing to the popular dislike for burials in that part of the church yard, there is no such aggregation. The west end of the north side has been shortened and an excavation made under it to admit a furnace chamber for the heating of the building. No new church however, could compensate us for the loss of this priceless relic of Plantagenet times. All that should be done to it is a faithful re-setting of every stone. To destroy it would be to efface a link that connections the chivalrous, pious days ... with the reign and subjects of Queen Victoria. It is the very centre to which the intervening generations in the district, in these six centuries, have brough their dead to be buried, their babes to be baptised and maidens to be married. Long may it continue to be so". (Wilson)

The parish records from 1678 record marriages, baptisms and deaths – many of the Ogles of Bothal and Lawsons of Longhirst. One wonders how many could be buried within the church. In the mid-Victorian period churches were being rebuilt in the grand style – for example at Mitford where a great tower with spire was added. Medieval buildings were mutilated, but Bothal was spared by the Hon and Rev W C Ellis. He was brother to Lord Howard de Walden and related to the family of the Duke of Portland. Like Morpeth, Bothal had an aristocratic rector. He restored the Church as suggested in the survey, and did not seek to advertise himself. His monument in the chancel is quite a simple tablet, recording that he was Rector of Bothal for 62 years – 1861 to 1923. The church might be regarded as his monument.

He built a new red brick rectory at Bothalhaugh over the river, which was reached from the church by a suspension bridge. He was a very keen gardener, and his gardens were much admired by visitors. Squires and parsons were often fond of hunting, but his sport was coursing, and he trained greyhounds for racing. A Bothal Coursing Club was established. In local affairs he played a prominent part. He was chairman of the Rural District Council and a member of the Morpeth Board of Guardians. In his later years he was saddened by the terrible toll of the First World War which brought about the loss of 35 young men of the parish, including his son Francis Bevis Ellis, Captain of the 10th Battalion Northumberland Fusiliers. A monumental cross outside the west end of the church records their names together with 22 who fell in the Second World War.

Planted by the cross and still growing is a weeping tree and another, a Japanese Maple, that burns red at the time of the Armistice on 11 November. Sometimes in a wild autumn the leaves are scattered early, but usually they are glowing at the time – a sight of beauty but also of sadness. Again, I think, the Rector was largely responsible for this memorial – certainly for promoting it. So Bothal has the graves of men who fell about the Castle and monuments to men who fell in Flanders fields or in dangerous waters. The majority of those who gave their lives from 1939-45 went to sea.

THE CHURCH OF ST ANDREW, BOTHAL

Hodgson speaks of the church as standing within a "bowshot" of the castle, and perhaps for that reason it did not need a defensive tower, or vicar's pele. A church reflects the time, wealth and circumstances of the place. In Border territories defensive works had priority and so there was not the wealth to be spent on churches as there was in Durham and Yorkshire, let alone the southern counties. Northumberland has no great towers, spires and elaborately ornamental churches. They are most often plain, severe and serviceable with no great expanses of coloured glass. There was often a western bell cote or bell gable. Churches are usually the oldest buildings in village or town and enshrine many centuries of history from the Saxon period to the present day. They were always in need of repair – sometimes modified and patched, sometimes demolished and rebuilt with tell-tale old stone re-used in the new building. Bothal is such an example and could be described as a typical Northumberland church, dating from Norman times or beyond.

Bothal Church. There was a Saxon church here, but what remains is medieval in structure.

But there was a church or churches before the Norman Conquest. When repairs were taking place in 1877, the chancel was excavated and fragments of old carved stone were found. Some of these were Anglo Saxon and showed that a church existed before the Normans. However, there was no proof that it was built of stone since the stones found were parts of crosses and gravestones. It was also discovered at this time, as was later found at Woodhorn, that there was once a shorter

chancel within the present limits of the building with an apsidal east end. There was some argument about this – the Rev Ellis considered it to be Norman and Canon McLeod considered it to be Saxon. This question cannot be settled; the Norman church could have followed the Saxon foundations.

There are a number of Norman churches in Northumberland, built in very much the same style and plan – consisting of nave and smaller chancel, separated by a rounded chancel arch. The windows are small and narrow, capped by a single stone – straight at the top and rounded underneath. The apertures are splayed to admit more light.

We first observe the west end of Bothal church. The bell cote takes three bells in arched shelters – one above two. The structured support is very like a chimney, and it is considered that this may go back to the 13th century. The west wall is supported by buttresses on either side of the bell cote support. There are also visible two narrow round headed windows. An ornamental cut has been made into each headstone at a later period. It can also be seen that aisles were added to the north and south of the church, shown by extensions of stonework. These aisles had steep sloping roofs which coincided with the steep sloping roof of the nave itself. At a later stage, as can be seen, the clerestories were added to the nave and the walls were raised. The roof was flattened as it appears now. The aisle walls were also raised to take flatter roofs – the cut of the old roof line can be seen across the stonework.

William Lawson of Longhirst died in 1858 aged 81 years, and was buried here like many Lawsons, but a few years later the Church of Saint John, Longhirst, was built, and so they were buried there. There are three medieval stone coffins of different sizes that probably came from the excavations within the church. Originally they would have had stone covers with ornamental crosses, and with a sword for a man, shears for a woman. At least one cover remains within the church. Pieces of carved stone can be seen built into the walls. No good stone was wasted, and it was easier to use old stone rather than quarry new stone. New stonework can be picked out. The maypole stone – a large round stone with a hole in the centre to take the pole when erected for May Day dancing – has been transferred inside. In Cromwellian times such baubles would be scrapped, and fonts were thrown out of the churches. The one outside Bothal Church came from the old chapel at Sheepwash. It was once used as a cattle trough in the demesne farmyard, near the old rectory.

Over the churchyard wall to the south was the old school and school house, begun by the Earl of Oxford about 1725. It has been converted into a house and the nearest school at Ashington is called "Bothal" Middle School. From the same wall one can see the clerestory rising above the roof line of the south aisle. There are four narrow Norman type windows with the old window heads that have received the same ornamental cuts as the west end windows. It can also be seen that the chancel now has a pointed roof as the nave formerly had. Before the restoration of the last century the chancel had a flat roof like the nave and the chancel gable stood

up on lonely isolation. The south side of the nave is approached by a 19th century porch. To the west of it is one square headed window, and to the east three windows of the same type and period. Three of them are original and monolithic – that is the window head is cut out of one piece of stone, whereas tracery is made up of a number of stone sections, correctly cut and carved. The windows have dripstones above, terminating in carved heads. The upper parts of the windows still retain fragments of medieval glass. Above the third window beyond the first buttress is a much eroded sundial, and on the buttress at the south-east corner of the nave is a scratch dial, also used for telling time. There are some 24 lines, like rays of the sun extending from the centre, where the lead is that held the piece of metal casting the shadow from the sun. The church is now somewhat shrouded in trees, but sunlight strikes upon and into the building.

From the large eastern window of the south aisle the light falls upon the alabaster tomb of Ralph, Lord Ogle and his wife. This eastern window, though larger and of three lights, has a monolithic window head, like its counterpart in the north aisle. In the chancel, just past the junction of nave and chancel, is a small low window, which reaches to ground level and has a wide splay. The other windows in the chancel, in both north and south walls, are of the long lancet type.

The eastern window of the chancel contains three lancets. The window it replaced now reposes in the vestry. It is similar to the east windows of the aisles, but a little more elaborate and constructed of separate pieces of stone. Hodgson's picture of the Church shows it in its original position in the east end. The square-headed windows seem to be 14th century, the style called Perpendicular. In the 13th century the chancel would have three lancet windows in the east end, and longer lancet windows were introduced in the 19th century to take the place of the one window transferred to the vestry.

The chancel has buttresses on each corner at the east end and two in between, separating the three lancets. Three lancet windows are visible in the north wall of the chancel – two have old stonework and the other is new. There are two old stone buttresses and one new one added at the restoration. It can be seen here that there is a lot of re-used stone, probably from the castle. A number of buildings within the walled enclosure were demolished. On the north side of the chancel the door was blocked only the priest's door on the south side is useable.

The north wall of the nave has re-used stone in building and the higher roof line can be seen with the flatter roof. The north door in the nave was blocked, probably at the time of the introduction of the heating furnace. It has two massive stones leaning together to make the doorhead, and it has been suggested that they date back to Saxon times. Stonework and building styles are difficult to date since similar styles are seen in towers and bastle houses over several centuries.

The north wall of the north aisle has buttresses at each end and one between. There are four square headed windows; three with monolithic stones and the fourth has been restored. Some stonework for this wall was moved from the original wall of the nave when the aisle was added, and the windows at that time would be of the

Norman round headed type as seen at the west end of the church.

The old water spouts have been replaced by more modern spouting. Both aisles and nave have the flatter type of roof, but the pointed roof has been restored to the chancel. A very good view of the church is obtained from the north. North of the church near the Smalridge monument is a tall cross resembling a village cross. This was set up about 1850 in memory of Lady Emily Cavendish, who was the wife of Rev Henry Hopwood, Rector of Bothal.

Having examined the exterior, it is time to venture inside the church through the modern porchway. Within the south-west corner of the nave was the brick vault of the Crows of Ashington, but this has been removed. The interior has changed substantially since the 16th century. The walls would have been painted with scenes from the lives of the Saints, St Christopher at the door, to welcome the traveller, a Doomsday scene over the chancel arch, depicting the Last Day and the different fates of those who were saved or damned. The rood screen, with Christ on the Cross, would separate the nave from the chancel. The chancel was strictly for the clergy and the laity saw what was going on through the woodwork or stonework of the screen. There were a number of images of saints and also a number of monuments to the important people of the past. The latest would be the Ogle monument in alabaster.

Inscriptions called upon the living to say prayers for the dead. A chantry had been established to say masses for the members of the Ogle family. Prayers for the dead were quite apart from the normal services.

In medieval times the church was the community centre; outside in the churchyard the cross was the place for bargaining. Church Ales were held in the churchyard – the medieval equivalent of garden parties – and there were festivities on Saints Days. The nave of the church was a place for general as well as religious meetings – the equivalent of the village hall – and there would be entertainments as well as services. Processions were held and not much seating was provided, only for the old and feeble.

With the Reformation in, the time of Edward VI, images were removed, stained glass broken and walls white-washed to cover superstitious paintings. Cuthbert, Lord Ogle, was thus able to inscribe his genealogy on the south wall of the chancel. It was at first in red, and it seems that years later the wall was white-washed and the inscription brought out in black. Much of the medieval painted glass was broken and only fragments remain. The windows of the chancel have been filled with Victorian period glass. It is quite likely that at the east ends of both the north and south aisles there were chapels that were separated by either timber or stone screens. In the Middle Ages everybody went to church, and the church told the time of day and the time of life. There were no bibles or prayer books; the service was in Latin and only the clergy had any form of service to consult. Very wealthy people could have Books of Hours, which were prayer books, lavishly illustrated. With Henry VIII came the English Bible and from Edward VI, the Book of Common Prayer in English. The Church itself can tell the story of changes in reli-

gion through the ages. Skulls and bones upon tombstones are reminders of the old Dance of Death, or symbols of mortality.

Only some of the stages of the development of the church can be seen from evidence above ground. The earliest churches are buried and evidence can only be discovered by excavation. Dowsing can reveal earlier structures, but can give no date. Some of the old stonework from Bothal Church restorations has been made into a wall to separate the vestry from the rest of the church. There are carved stones and pieces of arcading, difficult to fit into jigsaw puzzles of old churches. An old doorhead has been used for the vestry, and the window from the east end of the chancel has been re-erected against the west wall.

The south wall of the vestry is a piece of the north wall of the earliest visible church. The early Saxon-Norman churches were Romanesque in style with rounded windows. The nave was narrow, 20 feet within the walls and 25 feet with the walls in width. The length of the nave was usually twice the width and similar proportions applied to the chancel, which could have an apse at the east end. At Bothal the line of the north wall of the nave can be traced underneath the pillars to the chancel arch; in Norman times it would be rounded, but it has been raised and pointed at a later date. The apsidal east end of the chancel was revealed in 1877, but has been covered again.

The south wall of the church can be detected by a lump of masonry which was a wall and now serves to support an arch of the south aisle. The other pillar has also been carved from wall masonry. These show that the church was rectangular with no aisle. The north aisle was first established and the nave wall was replaced by four pointed arches with three octagonal pillars and responds to the west and east walls, which were ornamented. The arches were chamfered and little ornamental heads were added above the capitals of the pillars to the moulding. The original arches were altered probably in the 14th century when the walls above were raised to take the clerestory and the flattened roof.

In the north wall of the nave is a trefoil-headed recess and an awkward rectangular recess across the north east corner. These were probably used for statues or images. Standing in the middle of the nave one becomes aware of the what might be called inclinations and deviations. The pillars on both sides lean slightly outwards and alarmingly until one realises they have stood for five centuries. They eye suspects and measurements confirm that the nave is narrower at the west end than at the chancel arch. It seems that the south wall is out of alignment. In fact the south aisle has an odd look. The north aisle has four arches and the south only three. The explanation probably is that there was a south chapel which went as far as the large piece of old wall that supports the easternmost arch. There is a corresponding break in the wall outside from which part the wall of the aisle is added. The next pillar seems to have been carved out of a piece of solid wall. So the three wide arches open out into the south aisle, which lacks the symmetry of the north. The carved faces or head stops to the hood moulds of the south arches seem more primitive. Pevsner says – "The south arcade is a makeshift job with double chamfered arches dying into chunks of wall".

It is quite obvious that there was no great exactitude in medieval building, especially when alterations and repairs were being made. The north side of the chancel arch leans outwards and the masonry above is far from even in thickness. Some ornamental stonework built in at a higher level shows additions. Then chancel walls seem to have been increased in thickness.

The medieval glass in the aisles is fragmentary and confined to the window heads. The aisle windows are in the Perpendicular style. Three windows have in glass what might be called parts of buildings – crockets, pinnacles and spires. Other features are flowers which have symbolic or heraldic significance.

The north-east window contains most of the glass, which includes a heraldic shields and a picture of the Annunciation. Wilson wrote that first is shown an angel holding a scroll inscribed "Ave Gratia Plena, Dominus Tecum" (Hail (Mary) full of Grace, God be with you); and another scene above shows the Virgin at a prayer stool with a Bible and an inscription "Ecce Ancilla Domine" (behold the handmaiden of God). The glass is varied in colour and the window has fragments of buildings.

In the south aisle, the east window has a picture which Pevsner called the Coronation of the Virgin, but Evetts considered that it symbolised God Himself. In the second window can be seen the Arms of Bertram and the instruments of the Crucifixion "a cross with a crown of thorns twined around the intersection with nails standing out of the arms and of the foot, a spear on either side, a scourge on either side and a pillar on one side". (Pevsner) There are also fragments of glass in varying colours in each of the windows. Finally in the south-east corner of the nave is the Ogle monument of 1516. It has suffered from time and graffiti, but is very attractive. It has been moved and originally may have had some sort of canopy. The figures are of Ralph 3rd Lord Ogle and his wife Margaret Gascoigne, the knight in period armour and the lady in period dress with attendant dogs. Their coat of arms is below with supporters, a chained bull and a chained monkey. There are a number of well carved figures about the sides, the panels of which may have been moved. There are four ladies as weepers at the west end, four angels and three men at arms on the south side and five men at arms on the north side, partly hidden.

From the south chapel by the tomb we can see the squint or hagioscope to peer into the chancel. When the lights are not on in the church on a dull day, the beam of a torch will shine through the aperture to the candlesticks above the altar and the trefoil headed panels in dark wood on either side of the chancel appear like a gathering of hooded priests, seated at prayer. Above them subdued light comes in through the coloured glass of the windows restored in the time of Rev. Ellis. The chancel has an ordered uniformity that is lacking in the nave and interesting by contrast. In the south-east corner are the three sedilia or seats for the medieval priests. They have trefoil pointed heads on shafts with fillets with an adjacent piscina for the washing of communion plate. The panelling about the chancel has two apertures, through one of which the blocked north door can be seen, and the other

reveals a hole or recess within the masonry at the junction of nave and chancel. A torch will show considerable ornament on stone or alabaster that might have been connected with a monument, and there is hooding above. Also along the chancel wall within the gap can be seen two pairs of red lines – was this connected with the Ogle pedigree? And was there any connection with the south chapel in the nave or the Ogle tomb? The jutting piece of stonework above the tomb has been called a respond, but it may well have carried an image or lamp.

Another problem is the low side window in the south-west corner of the chancel. It is small, splayed and goes down the ground. Various suggestions have been made as to its purpose – for outside communications or for signalling the time to ring the sanctus bell. In other churches such have been called "Lepers' Windows." Another suggestion was that it was used for the dole of bread.

An interesting feature of the chancel is the Jacobean altar rails. Anne of Denmark, following her husband James VI of Scotland into England, stayed in Bothal Castle on the way, and may have visited the church.

Whereas the glass of the nave is fragmentary, that of the chancel is complete with nine lancet windows – three on each of the walls, the number having significance. Eight of these relate to saints and the central one in the east to Christ Himself. They are all fitted with colourful Victorian glass, which is now receiving greater appreciation.

The central east window shows Christ the Good Shepherd, and is to the memory of the Sharp family, who farmed in Pegswood for 200 years. On Christ's right is St Paul's window, to the memory of Thomas (d.1869) and Dorothy Bowden (d.1894). On his left is St Peter, in memory of Thomas Coxon (d.1893), who was for many years a churchwarden. On the north side of the chancel the windows show St Luke, St Jude and St James. The last is inscribed – "In memory of Herriet Georgina Caeline, Duchess of Sermonetta, who devoted herself to good work in this parish. This was dedicated by her brother, the Rector 1907. She died East Day 1906".

On the south side of the chancel St Mark's window is to the memory of Samuel and Grace Brewis; then St John and finally St Matthew "In memory of Arthur Storey, died 1899, aged 65, who was 40 years gamekeeper on the estate and his son Thomas who died 1898, aged 35, killed in a fall off a bicycle".

By contrast in the nave is the inscription to Anne, the wife of Dionisius Wilson translated from the Latin it reads:–

> *Beneath here lies Anna, the wife of Dionisius*
> *Wilson, who while she lived showed as much*
> *piety of life as probity of morals, and was*
> *not outshone by anyone of the same rank.*
> *Breathing her last breath, with her hands*
> *Stretched out and with her eyes raised,*
> *She calmly commended her soul to the*
> *hands of God on the second of April 1612 aged 22."*

Looking at the chancel with its modern high pitched roof, there is the difference of the low pitched roof of the nave and those of the aisles. These are old and medieval and in their time they were painted with shields and other adornment. In the last century the names of the families concerned could be deduced from the shields. After the Bothal Festival some years ago, several shields were made and are now on display round the walls.

There are still three bells in the turret and the earliest dates to 1615, inscribed "Gloria Deo Soli – Glory to God alone."

Bothal had another religious building, called the New Chapel of Our Lady. It is reached by a riverside path along the Wansbeck, west of the village, and always a popular walk. The valley is hung with trees and water pours over the weir that once provided power for the corn mill. The sluice gate and mill race are there, but the mill has been demolished, replaced by a yard that provides timber sheds and fences. Hodgson described the Chapel, which carried the arms of Bertram and Ogle. These were taken to the garden of Bothal Castle for safety. The Chapel was small, measuring 24 feet by 14 feet within the walls, and built of good freestone. It had become dilapidated and was overgrown. Later it was restored, but once again time and vandals have reduced it to ruin.

In medieval times it was the place of a holy man or hermit, who was visited by pilgrims. It was visited by Dr Turner, "the father of English botany", who wrote of a herb called "orobanche" that it was "so rare an herbe in England that I never saw it in all Englande but in Northumberland, where it is called the Newchapel flower".

BOTHAL CASTLE

The historian Watts, discussing the Border and the Rebellion of the North in 1569, wrote that there was "only one resident aristocrat in all Northumberland in 1586 – Cuthbert, Seventh Lord Ogle of Bothal, third son of the Sixth Earl of Shrewsbury. He died in 1597 and his son-in-law Edward Talbot took up residence in Bothal Castle." (Hodgson)

This was a time of great importance for the castle and there was a range of buildings within the walls. A survey was made for Lord Ogle in 1576. "To this manor of Bothoole belongest one castle, great chaulmer, parler, six bed chambers, a gallery, buttery, pantry larder, kitchen, bakehouse, brewhouse, a stable, a court called the yethouse, wharin there is a prison, a proter lodge and diverse faire chaulmering, an common stable and a tower called Blanke (Blanche) Toure: a gardine, ane nurice, chapel and a tour called Ogles Toure and a pastre with many other prettie beauldings here not specified, fair gardins and orchitts wharin growes all kind of herbes and floures and fine appiles, plumbes of all kynde, peers, damsellis, nuttes, wardons, cherries to the black and reede, wallnuttes and all licores verie fyne worth by all the yeare £20".

This gives a very good idea of the extent of the castle on the mound with its enclosing walls and towers. With all the buildings mentioned, obviously orchards

Bothal Castle consists of a strong gate house tower, commanding access to a walled enclosure and overlooking the old river crossing by Ford.

and garden areas were outside the defensive enclosure, which was divided into two courtyards. There were extra towers to add to the strength of the defences, though with the union of the two Kingdoms, in 1603, these were not now so necessary. Castles, however, came into use again for military purposes in the Civil War, which started some forty years after James had made his way southwards.

Sir William Cavendish, son of an Ogle heiress, later becoming the Duke of Newcastle, had a survey of the Bothal estate made in 1632. This shows a wooded area to the east on the Bank, and Bothal Park also wooded to the north. There is a large orchard area between the church and the river, and other such areas to the south and west of the castle. The map gives the divisions, field names and acreages of the whole estate.

The Civil War upset the Duke but after the return of Charles II in 1660, he recovered his estates. He was, however, more concerned with Ogle Castle, which was rebuilt and appears magnified in his book on horsemanship.

Buck's view in 1728 shows Bothal Castle to be very dilapidated, except for the gatehouse. Gaunt chimneys to roofless buildings show where the Great hall was on the west side and the brewery/bakehouse on the east side. The north-west tower still stands – this is probably the Blanche Tower, and a ruined building further north beyond the gatehouse on the site of the Ogle Tower has become stables.

Hodgson was impressed by the beauty of the trees, the river, the fields, gardens

and orchards and wished things could be "as they were in the days of Cuthbert, Lord Ogle and of good queen Bess". He continues – "The area within them and the slope to the west side, are usually occupied as gardens and orchards, the tenant of which lives on the ground floor of the great gateway, which has the entrance to it on both sides narrowed to the width of a common door: and that on the north covered by a porch of common walling and roofed with red tile". This is seen in the illustration from Scott's Border Antiquities, the Castle is roofless and the glassless windows gape.

In 1828 William Sample, agent to Greenwich Hospital, was appointed to manage the Bothal Estates for the Duke of Portland. Immediately he set about making improvements to the Gatehouse and other buildings. Repairs were to be in keeping with the style and quality of the existing structures. Materials from the Hall were used, supplemented from Ashington quarries. The entrance was cleared and a new stair put in, so that parts were made habitable. Scott's illustration shows the ruined gatehouse at the time of Hodgson's writing, with the blacksmith talking to a horseman.

The Directory of that time gives the name of the agent to the Duke of Portland as William Dickinson, who lived at Whiteside. George Cooper was the blacksmith and William Milburn, victualler and shopkeeper. Hodgson quoted Wallis's description "North-West of the building was formerly a tower, pulled down within the memory of a person yet living: part of its walls now support the cottage. Much of this venerable ruin has, as it is said, been demolished for the sake of its materials. The south front of this gate is beautifully mantled with ivy. In one of the towers is a staircase, leading into the different stories into which the building is divided. On the first, an elder tree has taken root in the rubbish, between the ribs of the gate. On the top of the westernmost tower, there is a small ash tree, which grows from between the chasms in the wall. Here, overlooking the battlements are two figures, one over the gate, the other over the north west tower, but so defaced by time and weather as to render it impossible to distinguish what they were intended to represent. The groove for the portcullis is still visible". (Hodgson)

One of the figures held a horn and the other a large stone as if to hurl at some attacker. The gatehouse dates from the middle of the 14th century, after Edward III, in 1343, had granted Sir Robert Bertram a licence to crenellate his mansion or hall at Bothal. It has been suggested that a Norman motte and bailey Castle replaced the Saxon Hall but there is no proof.

Modern research has shown that the Normans did make "ring" defences or earthworks enclosing an area without the construction of a mound. The present site of Bothal Castle is the obvious place for such a fortified enclosure with hall. It rises above the immediate countryside, and is defended on one side by the river. The other sides would be moated, and in the present area of entrance there would be a ditch with a drawbridge. The stone curtain walls are difficult to date since there is a mixture of stonework, and the masonry differs in thickness. There would be stone walls before the gatehouse was built. When it was built a considerable force was

necessary to defend the area against Scottish attacks. There was a great hall within the walled area, but any details would need excavation. It is worth while looking at the castle from various directions – from the western approach, when the full extent of the curtain walls, the gatehouse and the Sample additions can be seen, then there is the front view of the gatehouse and the path to the river below the castle in what was probably the moat. The castle overlooks the river crossing, once a ford and now stepping stones, but there is a hanging bridge over the river to Bothalhaugh Gardens and Rectory (now Kind Care Kennels). By this way Rev Ellis came to church, and the castle can be viewed from the higher bank. Another view can be obtained from the top of Bothal Bank or the footpath leading to Sheepwash, where the old rectory was.

The Gatehouse provided the lord's residence and accommodation was duplicated in the hall for retainers. The Gatehouse gave control of the whole area, and was intended to give a great impression whether to visitor or attacker. Sir Robert Ogle had served the King well and Edward III himself was a great fighter. In his time there was stress on the ideals of knighthood and chivalry. King Arthur was very much admired. Chronicles and ballads gave something of the romance of war.

The main bulk of the gatehouse measures about 40 feet by 30 feet. On either side of the entrance a semi-octagonal turret extends 15 feet outwards from the gate itself, so that it is well covered from above. The turrets are projected beyond the walls. The gatehouse faces north and there is a fine ornamental window to the second floor. It rises high and is made very impressive by a series of ornamental shields, in honour of the King, Bothal and the knights who bore these arms in war. Pride of place goes to Edward III, Victor of Crecy and Poitiers in France. His shield carried the three lions of England and the Fleur de Lys of France, showing his claim to that crown. The Black Prince's shield is on his right and Lord Wake of Lydel in Cumberland on his left. Others in order are Aton of Alnwick, Greystock of Morpeth, Percy of Alnwick, Bertram of Bothal, Darcy, Conyers and Felton. On the west turret are the arms of Delaval, Scargill, Horsley and Ogle.

Under this impressive array is the entrance by a tunnel – vaulted passage 33 feet long and 12 feet wide. Above were three openings or "murder holes", through which things could be showered on attackers. They could also be used for servicing the apartments above, saving an awkward journey by the spiral stairs. There were small apartments in the basement at either side of the entrance passage. These were used as guardrooms, stores and a prison. There was a second gate defending the inner courtyard and a spiral stair in the south-west corner of the gatehouse, giving access to the apartments and battlements.

Hodgson was provided with information by Mr Lawson of Longhirst, who at that time was having a grand house built to the design of John Dobson. Lawson was knowledgeable about architecture, but the castle was in such a ruinous state that it was difficult to sort out.

He says – "Opposite to these stairs, on the other side of the gateway, is a large hall". By the winding stairs "we entered the state room above the gateway".

(Hodgson) This measured 25 feet by 17 feet within thick walls (seven feet), and had four windows, the largest being on the north side. The window recess had stone benches, which could seat six persons. From the windows were fine views of the village, the church and the Wansbeck. At each corner, doors led to the chambers within the projecting towers, each measuring 11 feet by seven feet and lit by loopholes. The fireplace was in the east wall of the main apartment. The upper levels were impossible to sort out because of the ruinous condition, but the battlements could be reached and the strange figures examined. White, in 1847, wrote that the village was "much improved within the last few years, the houses have been nearly all rebuilt", but the castle was still ruinous.

However, during the next years the gatehouse was rebuilt and new apartments were added to the north. A fine decorated window and a fireplace were brought from Cockle Park, which the Duke of Portland owned.

The spiral stair at Bothal ended with an umbrella vault, with a door leading to the battlements. Bates considered that the masons who built the gatehouse were also at Prudhoe Castle, and he gave grudging approval to the 19th century restoration.

The battlements are interesting – the merlons of masonry twice as wide as the embrasures (openings), in which the hinge holes for the shutters can be seen. The wooden shutters were raised to fire against the enemy and smartly dropped against a reply. From the battlements it would be perfectly possible to communicate with other fortifications.

At the present time Bothal Castle is leased to Welwyn Electronics, and used to provide hospitality for their commercial visitors. Hogson hoped that "the profits of the barony be gain employed in bidding the vivifying voice of hospitality to be heard within the castle walls", as they were in olden times, and so it is.

CHAPTER VIII: COAL – MINED AND OPENCAST

In this neighbourhood the most significant changes have been in the methods of winning coal. Today instead of multiple pyramid spoil heaps from coal pits, a large area is dominated by a huge mound within a baffle bank, to limit the noise and dust from excavations. Such is the Butterwell mound and in late October 1991, an industrial monument in the shape of the dragline "Big Geordie" appeared. This

Big Geordie, a gigantic dragline excavator, has reached retirement stage after 22 years of service. It now rests at Butterwell.

monster moved from the Sisters site at Widdrington in 1976, and has worked continuously at Butterwell since that time, removing huge amounts of overburden to reveal the seams of coal. The site covers 2,000 acres and as excavation proceeds the land is restored to agricultural use with trees and hedges planted and drainage provided. The topsoil and subsoil are removed systematically and set aside for the final stages of renewal. The rock moved by excavators is also consolidated by them, and it is returned by dump trucks into the void. So far some 750 acres have been restored to grassland and tillage, with more being added every day. It is estimated that some 13 million tonnes of good coal will be obtained from the site in 28 seams. Coal had been mined from the upper levels formerly, but the present excavations go down to 145 metres. It is quite an astounding picture to see as many as seven seams of coal at different levels across the face of the rock. Holes are drilled vertically into the rock and explosives introduced to fracture it. The upper layers of

rock are excavated by face shovels and the lower by dragline. Now Big Geordie has reached his limit and the remaining area has to be cleared by face shovels. Big Cat dumptrucks can move 170 tonnes of rock at a time and medium sized ones 85 tonnes. The coal is carried in 20 ton capacity road type lorries by site roads to the screening plant. Here the coal is crushed, screened and blended to be taken away by rail or road. Roughly one third goes to industry, one third to power stations and one third is exported.

While Butterwell is reaching its final stages, another site has been opened at Stobswood. Here a new dragline, bigger than Big Geordie named, "Ace of Spades" is in operation. Opencast mining is a controversial subject, but it does seem that quite often the land is restored to a better state than it was, especially where the area has been mined before leaving humps, water-logged hollows and subsidence. British Coal has done a great deal to help wild life and to provide recreational facilities after opencast workings in the form of country parks, lakes and plantations. A good example is the Queen Elizabeth II Park at Woodhorn; and Druridge Bay Country Park has been developed from opencast workings. The old mining spoil heaps have also been landscaped as at Pegswood and Barrington.

The other side of the picture is that in the 30 years since the nationalisation of coal in 1947, some 60 coal pits in Northumberland and 117 in Durham have been closed. Most of the land mining in Northumberland is from opencast, but there are small private mines, as at Shadfen.

North Seaton colliery was closed in 1961, Stobswood in 1965, Choppington A & B in 1966, Newbiggin in 1967, Cambois and Linton in 1968, Pegswood and Longhirst in 1969 and Netherton in 1974, while Bedlington lost all its pits. It is difficult now to realise the impact that coal had on houses and transport, with smoking chimneys and steam trains. Perhaps the extent of the change is epitomised by Ashington – early in the last century a farm and a few cottages, after 1850 mushroom growth into what has been called the largest colliery village in the country, twice as big as Morpeth town. Now there is no colliery at Ashington, where once was one of the largest in the country. The first pit here was called "Fell 'em doon", more politely Felham Down. This might describe both the fate of the trees, for it was a much wooded area, and the coalpits that followed into oblivion.

Coal is still of great importance in the area, supplying the power station at Woodhorn for Alcan Aluminium Works and to North Blyth power station for supplying electricity to the area. Coal trains and waggons are continually plying backwards and forwards across the viaducts and bridges. Blyth staithes are no longer used, but coal ships are still loaded at Bates.

SHEEPWASH AND THE BISHOPRIC

At this stage we may wander over the river at Sheepwash, which was the tidal limit of the Wansbeck, and could be navigated up to here by small craft. There were plans to make the Wansbeck into a canal as far as Morpeth, but nothing came of it and waggonways were used instead. The area south of the river was not

Sheepwash. In the foreground is seen the weir for a mill. On the bank the Old Rectory for Bothal and new housing lie on the site of the medieval hospital.

regarded as part of Northumberland till 1844. Previously it was regarded as part of Durham as belonging to the Bishop, hence it was called Bedlingtonshire. North of the Wansbeck in Pegswood and Ashington the social centres are clubs, but south of the river is a fine selection of pubs – the Angler's Arms and the Shakespeare at Sheepwash, the Queen's Head at Guide Post, the Cherry Tree and Half Moon at Stakeford as well as the Lord Barrington, the wealthy family that provided a Bishop. There is the Traveller's Rest at Choppington, where Thomas Burt came to live in 1860; and he was married at Bedlington. He worked down Choppington Pit and appreciated the countryside: when he had time he went for walks across the fields.

"The wellwooded valley of the Wansbeck was within an easy stroll. From Morpeth to the sea, notably at Bothal and Sheepwash there were pictures of sylvan beauty which could be hard to match in any part of the world. After my day's work in the pit was over and I had rested awhile, thither did I often wander book in hand, on summer afternoon". (Burt)

In time he became secretary of the local Miners' Union and in 1874 was elected MP for Morpeth, serving the constituency for more than 40 years. It included Bedlington, which had belonged to the Bishop. Bedlingtonshire was included in the Boldon Book 1183, a survey of the properties of the Bishopric, recording the obligations of the tenants in both services and payments.

"West Sleekburn returns 6½ marks (£4:6s:8d) of rent, carries the writs of the Lord Bishop as far as the Tweed (Norham), goes on massions, and does court duty

and the township prepares the mill and the pond, each household with one man, and carry loads as far as Newcastle and as far as Fenwick (port of Islandshire) while on their own journeys and they enclose the court and they cover the hall (at Bedlington), and prepare the fishery like the men of Bedlington." (Boldon)

Services could be converted to payments, one mark being worth 2/3 of £1.

Turkhill paid 12 hens to the Bishop and Patrick one pound of pepper (quite valuable). The Boldon Book reports, "The fishery of Cambois is leased out to Adam of Cambois and his heirs for 3 shillings a year free & exempt... The mills of Bedlingtonshire return 24 marks". Tenants had to keep the Bishop's fishponds in repair as well as his mills and millponds.

At this time coal was used to evaporate brine in salt pans, to supply both the Bishop and the Abbeys of Newminster and Tynemouth. The monks did not work in mines themselves, but used lay brothers or other workers to do the heavy work.

The Bishop's tower and hall at Bedlington were knocked down in recent years and replaced by the Council Offices. At Cambois in medieval times there was a house for the Bishop's agent and a chapel, which was embodied in the farm buildings of what has now become The Buccaneer Public House at the mouth of the Wansbeck.

CAMBOIS

Hutchinson wrote in 1778 – " Cambois at the mouth of the river Wansbeck, haven with two quays on the north shore for small vessels about 30 tons burthen, employed in the export of corn and grindstones and importing timber. Many lime boats from adjacent coasts resort to this place. The cliffs by the sea called Hawk's Heugh are rude and majestic. There is a cavern towards the north end, well known to smugglers".

Wallis gives more details. The river here "is actually called Cambois Water & Cambois Harbour. It is navigable to the Stakeford for small vessels of about 30 tons burthen. There are 2 keys on the north side: one called the Low and the other the High Key: the latter on the estate of Sir Thomas Clavering Bart., a great export of corn and grindstones from them & a considerable import of Norway timber and deals: and of limestone from Beadnell & Sunderland in boats. Near a mile from the harbour's mouth is a range of cliffs called Hawk's Heugh from its being a recess of hawks in the breeding season; ravens also and other birds frequenting it. Towards the north end is a cavern, very large, with an aperture at the top, usually called by the mine men Self Opens: the refuge of foxes and badgers in their distress by the chace.

"A little further north, by a grindstone quarry on the sea banks, called Spittal quarry, an urn was found by workmen unroofing the quarry, placed between 4 stones set edgeways with a coverstone, at the depth of 3 feet from the surface: the urn of red earth, small, bellied without any ornaments, left by the incurious finders among the rubbish." It was a grave and an urn of probably a Bronze Age man, living about 1500 BC. Several other "cists" have been exposed.

Wheatley's Ferry at the mouth of the Wansbeck was the old crossing of the river; the ferryman hauling on a wire rope.

Wansbeck mouth tended to decline as a port and Blyth assumed greater importance. The Ridleys had acquired much land in this area and Cambois Farm shows the quality of the buildings. Cambois was also a seaside resort and we read of the Ridleys paying visits. Lady Cecilia wrote in September 1844 – "Today I have been all the way to the sea at Cambois, where I walked wondrously, made a very trumpery sketch and found several new flowers. Tomorrow I hope to go to Morpeth" "As we were sitting on the beach by the sea an old man came up and gave Matt a pat with his stick across the shoulders and then sat down with us and talked familiarly. He tried to make out where we came from, and at last asked me if I knew who the gentleman was. I said, "I believe Sir Matthew Ridley." "Oh no it can't be," said he, "one of his servants you mean."

Little Matt was her son and Sir Matthew her husband.

"The village contains 16 houses, and some large granaries, the latter of which were erected during the late war", (Parson) ending in 1815. The public house then was the Saracen's Head. Armstrong's map shows the houses and the ferry. Cambois was written Cambois then and is pronounced 'Cammus', which confuses strangers. The basic meaning is a curve, which can be applied to a bay or hill, as Cambo.

Another local name which has caused merriment is 'Boca Chica', the name given to a local house. Seamen serving under Admiral Vernon at the Siege of

Cartagena (1741), liked the name given to the harbour there – "little mouth" and it was given a local connection on their return. It has since disappeared under the Power Station coal deposits.

John Wallace in 1869 was excited by the developments at Cambois. "The new winning of the Cowpen Coal Company close to this village, has broken the quiet of centuries. On the links a great number of houses has been erected, and are occupied by a busy population...

The Colliery is in full operation, being fitted up with the latest and most approved appliances for raising coal and pumping water." The winding engine could raise 1400 tons of coal in 12 hours. The pumping engine pumped 300 gallons a minute, a distance of 250 yards.

"A railway has been made from the pit to the link end, where the coals are put on board the vessels with the greatest facility. At one of the staithes screw colliers can take in coals from two spouts simultaneously. The first shipment of Cambois coals took place 27 June 1867." (Wallace)

Cambois Colliery closed in 1968; North Blyth staithes remain but are no longer used. A wheel from the colliery, made in Tamworth, now adorns Queen Elizabeth II Park on the other side of the river. Vald Birn factory is on the colliery site and the colliery is remembered by a little pit tub.

The mouth of the Wansbeck changes constantly with the impact of the sea. Southwards are Blyth South Harbour, Alcan loading terminal, corn and coal facilities and four great chimneys of the power station. There is a long stretch of sand, but the cliffs are continually eroded as at Newbiggin where the Church of St Bartholomew stands on the headland, as a landmark for ships. Adjacent to it is a caravan park and another at Sandy Bay. The sands have so piled up at Wansbeck mouth that at low tide it is possible to cross the river on foot. It is now a difficult entrance for boats since the weir holding the water for the Riverside Park, prevents the flushing of the entrance. Boats can only cross the bar at high tide for a very short time and the waves may make navigation difficult. But it is interesting to look round the remains of the old harbour, while traffic whizzes by on the spine road. A lot of boats remain within the maritime park, but there is a lock to allow access and exit. It is pleasant to walk along the river back as far as Sheepwash bridge. Once there was a stone bridge with four arches, but it was damaged in 1869. At present there are two iron bridges – one for traffic and the other for pedestrians.

CHAPTER IX: ASHINGTON

Ashington was once only a farmhouse and cottages. A description of 1777 runs "Ashington which was one of the manors of the Barony of Bothal, now belongs to George Sandiford Crowe Esq. It stands on an eminence, well sheltered with tall forest trees: a fine view from it of the sea, also of Seaton Delaval and Bebside through the openings in the plantations: the grounds sloping down regularly to the bank of oaks by the river Wansbeck, freestone rocks conspicuous through them under which is a fine grass area of a mile in length by the river, which for all its length forms a most beautiful serpentine canal, a bank of oaks on the opposite side. On the west side of a streamlet called the Den Burn, by a grindstone quarry the Wansbeck makes a flexure, where is a beautiful slope, now in tillage shaded by spreading oaks and other timber on all sides but the south, the river making another flexure a little to the west of it, crossed by the Sheepwash bridge in sight: a boat in it for the use of a salmon fishery. Mr Crowe's extent of ground by the river from within a small field's length of the bridge or the rectory glebe, to the Stakeford, east is about a mile and a half measured, thus beautifully chequered with wood, rock and river scenery, a footwalk by the river the whole length." Much of this still applies. The writer added – "The Black Close, belonging to his Grace, the Duke of Portland, where is a coal work, a steith and a small fire engine so contrived as to fill a large bason with salt water from a small reservoir below, overflowed by the tides, for the use of a salt work and also to draw off water from the colliery". (Hutchinson)

Wallace informs us that there were salt pans at Cowpen, Cambois and Sleekburn. "The labour in making salt was chiefly done by females: they pumped the water, wheeled the coals in barrows, and shovelled the coals in firing the pans. Their wages were small, which they eked out by teasing oakum and pilfering small quantities of salt, which with the duty then levied upon it made it of considerable value".

The duty on salt was £30 per ton, when the selling price was £34:10s per ton, so there was much inducement to illicit trade and smuggling. There were many secret cauldrons for evaporating brine, just as there were illicit whisky stills, and smuggling was rife. The introduction of measures of free trade and reduction of duties led to a decline in smuggling and the domestic manufacture of salt discontinued. The fire engine above was a steam engine, first used for pumping water from mines, and there were many in this county.

Ashington was purchased by the Duke of Portland. The farm house is well built in Georgian style and has a fine collection of buildings. In front of the house across the road were large walled gardens. Older maps show that to the west was Sparrow House, once the property of George Sandiford Crowe, but now no more. Above the door of Ashington farmhouse is a fine coat of arms, probably of the Crowe family. Was "sparrow" for the other house a local pun? It has been demolished and a magpie nests there. I am told that the coat of arms is that of Douglas.

Ashington Farm consists of a group of fine stone buildings, overlooking the Wansbeck.

There is a footpath across the fields to the Wansbeck Riverside Park, where there are some magnificent old trees which mask the old quarry workings. Eastwards can be seen areas of grassland with bushes, the bridges and the approach to the sea. Modern Ashington, now a town rather than a village or farm spreads to the north. It was the result of the development of a number of coalpits in the area. Tomlinson wrote in 1888 – "Ashington, a large colliery village, somewhat less ugly than the majority of colliery villages, some of the later built rows, being comfortable, substantial & even attractive". It was regarded as a model village of the time. The houses were built in rows facing south and at the back was a 20 feet wide road with lavatories and coalhouses on the other side. It was separated by a seven feet high wall from the 30 yards long gardens of the next row. Ten miles of tramway were built for trains to bring coal and carry away refuse.

Chester Armstrong came in 1881 as a boy, when his father had to leave employment in Nenthead in a lead smelter because of his health. Those employed in lead mines and lead works tended to think themselves a cut above the colliers or coal miners, who were rough and hard drinking. His family were Primitive Methodists and so for that matter were many coal miners. He wrote – "In 1881 Ashington was but a colliery village, extending no further east than the manager's house at the end of the front row & limited on the west by the oldest part of the colliery. Looking eastward from the manager's house, the land was almost bare as far as Woodhorn village, which lies midway between Ashington & Newbiggin by the Sea, save the railway station, which had just previously been built: a farmstead

held by Mr Nixon: and two cottages and what was known as Low Hirst, comprising an ancient castle and a few low cottages adjoining".

Hirst Castle was knocked down in 1908 for the widening of the road and the Hirst area developed more colliery rows than Ashington, which became an umbrella name to cover the whole area. The Ordnance Survey map of the 1880s shows the colliery with 10 rows to the south of it. On the southern fringe of building from east to west were the Miners' Hall, Schools, Methodist Chapel, Portland Arms Hotel, the Vicarage and Holy Sepulchre Church with another Methodist Chapel near and more schools.

Railway lines and sidings are the northern limit with a railway leading to a junction with the main line north of Pegswood. In recent times the direct road from Pegswood to Ashington has taken this route. Previously the main road was through Bothal involving steep climbs and sharp bends. The pools and holes about Coneygarth show the old activities of quarrying, mining and digging clay for the brick and tile works, which were always associated with collieries.

Bulmer's account of 1888 reads – "The colliery, known as Ashington colliery, is situated in Bothal Demesne, about a mile north of the Wansbeck. The output from the two pits in operation is about 2,000 tons a day. At the Bothal pit, where the Grey seam is wrought, the coal is reached at 36 fathoms. The seam has a section of four feet of clean coal. The Low Main seam, which here lies at a depth of 94 fathoms is worked at the Carl pit. The sections of this seam shows three feet six inches, band five inches then coal one foot three inches. both these seams rank high class seam coal.

In close proximity to the above pits and connected with them by a gangway is the new "Duke" pit, which is sunk to the Low Main seam. This pit adds 1,000 tons per day to the output and gives employment to 600 or 700 additional hands. At present 2,000 men and boys are employed. In addition to the colliery, the Ashington Coal Company also farms about 900 acres of land belonging to the Duke of Portland. (Sparrow House was one of the their farms.) This chiefly laid down in meadow, to furnish hay for the large stud of ponies and horses used in and about the pits: and from the dairy the company supply the greater part of the workmen with milk".

"The village of Ashington, which has risen up for the accommodation of the colliers, is quite a model pit village. The houses are of superior class & every attention has been paid to the sanitary arrangements, water supply etc. There are now 665 cottages arranged in eleven rows & between each row a tramway, by means of which fire coal is supplied to each household & the contents of the ashpits systematically & economically removed.

Another feature which might be usefully copied elsewhere is that the sale of intoxicating liquors is not permitted: the result is that there is very little drunkenness & one policeman suffices for a population of nearly 4,000. Schools (Bothal National Schools) for the accommodation of 1,000 children have been erected by

the Company & a large & efficient staff of teachers are maintained." (Bulmer) (The main mixed school had headmaster, five assistant masters and four assistant mistresses. The Infant's school had headmistress and four assistant mistresses.)

Chester Armstrong became weighman at Carl pit – he hated the underground work, and spent years working above ground. He wrote of the extensions of Ashington – "Long rows or street, some of them more than a mile in length, for the most part running parallel to each other & so close together as to be severely congested, compared with the older part of Ashington." (Armstrong) He found it ironical that the streets should be given the names of trees and shrubs – Hawthorn Road, Sycamore Street, Laburnum Terrace and Acacia Terrace. Some rows are said to be the longest in the country.

The setting up of the first hotels in Ashington (which were public houses) caused very much concern and was strongly opposed by temperance people and Nonconformist denominations. In spite of strong opposition, licences were granted, the argument being that it was necessary for important persons such as coal owners and visitors. The most impressive buildings of this kind erected were the Portland Hotel and the Grand Hotel, described as "well appointed hostelries". Another notable building was the Miners Hall, built 1894-6, where political meetings were held and lectures given. It opened in 1896, providing a building large enough for public entertainment and cultural activities. It was used for many years as a theatre and cinema.

The Harmonica Hall was erected in 1897 and here the Ashington Amateur orchestral Society met. The Mechanics Institute, a social and educational centre had a library, reading room and billiards room. Music could be provided by several brass bands. A Literary and Debating Society was established. One active member was Ebby Edwards, who became MP for Morpeth and was Secretary for the Miners Federation of Great Britain.

The Methodist and Presbyterian Churches played a prominent part in the life of Ashington as did the Catholic Church St Aidan's (1905).

Another institution of the greatest importance for material welfare was the Co-operative Society (or Societies, since there was some amalgamation). Ashington has been written about as "The Pit and the Store", dominating underground and above ground respectively.

The Co-operative Society provided educational assistance to its members, reaching out as far as Ruskin College or Stanford Hall. Chester Armstrong was one of the Management Committee. The Society extended to ten different departments in 1919, and in 1924 were building new offices and shopping arcade in classical style with Ionic pillars, cornices and friezes. This is perhaps the best building in Ashington and should be scheduled.

Armstrong wrote of the official opening "of the imposing block of arcaded premises erected by the Ashington Industrial Co-operative Society. This ceremony took place early in May 1926. Despite the unpropitious events of the General

The headquarters of Ashington Co-operative Society, built in the grand style, is the most imposing structure of the town.

Strike & the coal trade stoppage, the occasion was auspicious & quite in keeping with local Co-operative enterprise. Mr William Ross the president of the society performing the opening ceremony, while I had the honour of presiding".

Ashington was under Morpeth Rural District Council until 1896 when it became an Urban District Council, including Hirst and parts of Sheepwash and Bothal Demesne. It was divided into two wards and governed by UDC of 18 members, nine from Ashington and nine from Hirst. From 1888 it had separated from Bothal ecclesiastically and included parts of Bothal Demesne and Sheepwash, where an old church had been. The new church in Ashington was given the same dedication, the Holy Sepulchre. The Church in Norman and Early English style was consecrated in 1887 and aisles were added later. It could seat 750 people.

The new Council Chambers were built and opened in 1912, when the Chairman invited Councillors and their friends to a dinner at the Portland Hotel. The seal of the local authority shows the Duke Pit Heapstead and the motto "Labor Omnia Vincit", (Labour Conquers All).

Certainly this applies politically since Ashington has been represented by a line of Labour MPs and Morpeth has been swallowed in the constituency.

Over a century Ashington has had many difficult problems to overcome. At first there were poor water supply, sanitation and sewage disposal made acute by such a rapidly growing population. Village solutions to these problems were use-

less in what was really a town. Water and sewage seeped into the local streams and then the Wansbeck. In 1927 a drainage scheme was formulated and carried out, electric lighting was introduced and Tynemouth Water Company provided the necessary supply of water. Coal fires in homes, mines, factories and on the railways meant considerable air pollution and badly blackened buildings. Now with much household heating by electricity, gas and oil, only a few coal fired houses can illustrate the "reek" of the old pit villages.

The Ashington Coal Company among other things provided rail transport between its collieries and colliery villages, including Pegswood, Linton and Ellington. Miners travelled to and from work in rail carriages and their families could also use this transport – at first free, but later a small charge was made. Excursions were also provided for officials and workers with their families. The local council and the Coal Company both helped in the provision of playing fields and recreational areas, such as parks.

The churches also provided for their members particularly the Methodists, who developed strongly in mining communities. Miners came into Ashington from the lead mines of Allendale and elsewhere and from other parts of the country. The great achievement in Ashington was the construction of the Methodist Central Hall, a fine building with a dome and perhaps the best in Ashington. It was opened in 1924 with great ceremony for services and meetings. Unfortunately in recent years the building went out of use and was demolished.

An official guide states – "Ashington is a place of people rather than buildings, of character packed humanity rather than historical traditions, a place where people matter. Coal made the town famed as "the largest mining village of the world", but today it is soccer famous as the birthplace of Bobby and Jack Charlton, the only brothers to appear in an England World Cup winning team (1966). They have given Ashington a unique distinction which may never be repeated in the annals of soccer". (Robson)

Another international star was Jackie Milburn, who played for Newcastle and whose story appeared on TV. Cissie Charlton (nee Milburn), the mother of Jack and Bobby, had four brothers who all played in First Division Football. Her autobiography entitled *Cissie* is good reading and provides an interesting picture of family life in the area as well as the effects of football upon it. Ashington still has very useful cricket and football teams.

From here emerged distinguished figures in the world of music such as Sheila Armstrong and Janice Cairns. Concerts are still frequently provided, though with the decline of the mining industry, the number of brass bands has diminished.

CHAPTER X: DISTRICT OF WANSBECK

In 1974 there occurred another great change, which makes it even more difficult to define Ashington and Wansbeck. The district Wansbeck was formed by the amalgamation of three neighbouring areas of Ashington, Newbiggin and Bedlingtonshire, formerly belonging to the Bishopric and also situated on the Blyth. So Bedlington is omitted from this book as is Ponteland which is by the River Pont. More than 60,000 people inhabit the district of Wansbeck, which proclaims its boundaries by stating that it is a nuclear free area. Coal is very much opposed to a rival form of power, but in its time coal has produced massive pollution and damage to the landscape.

An official publication runs – "At one time 15 collieries were operating in Wansbeck and the district could rightly justify its claim to be "King Coal" in North East England."

Curiously now the only colliery in Wansbeck is Woodburn Mining Museum. Ellington-Lynemouth is in Castle Morpeth and the Alcan Smelter and Power Station are in Wansbeck. The north bank of the Blyth is the boundary of Wansbeck district and includes the Alcan Terminal, from which the smelter is supplied by rail.

Re-organisation of local government increased the extent of the problems of Wansbeck District, since they were the same in each area – mines that had been closed and industrial dereliction. These were tackled in an encouraging way, but only some examples can be quoted.

The area was dotted with pit heap mountains and colliery waste tips. Most of these have been levelled and grassed over or returned to cultivation. Some low mounds have been planted with trees. The best example is the Ashington-Woodhorn mountain heap of blackness, which formerly dominated the landscape. It was about a mile long and a quarter of a mile wide and contained some ten million cubic metres of waste. This was moved and fashioned into gently rounded humps and level fields, becoming attractive parkland. The work cost three million pounds which was provided mainly by the Government and carried out by the NCC Reclamation Unit.

Part of the scheme was Queen Elizabeth II Silver Jubilee Country Park, officially opened in 1979 by the Queen Mother. There is a 40 acre lake which is used for water sports, and a Lakeside Hotel. The dominating single feature is the winding wheel from Cambois Colliery, surprisingly large when set up at ground level. Close by, Wansbeck Business Park has been developed to provide business units in an attractive woodland site. In other mining areas parks have been developed and also extensive industrial estates, where men of the mines could obtain different employment.

The Wansbeck Riverside Park has already been mentioned. This area had suffered from neglect and rubbish dumping, but still contained attractive parts. In the

1970s its potential was realised and measures were taken to improve the situation. The river banks were strengthened to prevent flooding and paths were developed. Some overgrowth was cleared. Playground and picnic areas were provided. A weir was constructed near the sea to maintain a continuous water level for water sports. A caravan site and camping ground were provided. In addition there are walks and nature trails along two miles of riverside. There are resident swans and shelducks are being encouraged to nest. Cormorants come up river to fish. The railway viaduct, once of timber like the staithes, is now of iron with timber-like structure. It is used entirely for industrial traffic.

There are now extensive housing developments above the riverside and the pattern is very different from the long rows of the old Ashington. The pattern is repeated in the other modern housing developments, which can be seen on a map or aerial photograph. Ashington had a hospital in 1915, extended during the war and after so that it became an important centre for medical care to a large part of Northumberland. This has now been replaced by a much larger up to date establishment.

The other institution that should be mentioned is the former Mining Institute, which developed into the seven storey Northumberland County Technical College. It provided for full time and part time students with day release studies. Now called Northumberland College it is the largest education institution in the County with some 4,000 students. A Business Centre is part of the development on the colliery site.

Another notable development was the Ashington Leisure Centre. The Miners Welfare had long provided facilities including swimming baths. In 1973 the Miners Welfare and town council formed a trust to develop new leisure facilities on the site. A two court sports hall and indoor bowling green were constructed and the activities of the Institute were extended. A second phase followed with swimming pool, squash courts and training rooms. The result was that badminton, basket ball and wrestling could be staged. Various displays were arranged and the main hall, with seating for 900 people, was the venue for a range of concerts.

MidNAG (the Mid Northumberland Arts Group) helps to provide artistic entertainment. Plays and operas are put on and its activities are extended to Morpeth and Newbiggin. It is heavily involved in staging the annual Ashington Festival – a fortnight of music, dancing, sports, exhibitions and drama. MidNAG is also responsible for a number of publications on art and poetry, and travelling exhibitions, including both photographic and artistic records. These exhibitions are held locally, travel round the county and to other parts of the country. Woodhorn Church Museum has regular exhibitions and displays of country crafts.

CHAPTER XI: WOODHORN COLLIERY MUSEUM

At the north-east tip of Ashington beyond the site of the demolished Hirst Castle are Woodhorn villas, and over the railway in the Queen Elizabeth Country Park is the Woodhorn Mining Museum, which was officially opened by Neil Kinnock. It occupies the site and some of the buildings of the old colliery. The work of sinking the shafts there began in 1894, and three years later the first coal was brought up. A monument has been re-erected at the Museum to 13 miners, who were killed in the disaster of 13 August 1916, a reminder of how dangerous mining was and still is. The pit head with winding wheels has been retained, but the tall brick-built chimney has been demolished. Here was the last pit to use steam power in the Northumberland and Durham coalfield. This part of the old mine is not open to the public, but gives a good idea of the pit head equipment and buildings, with two engine houses and two pairs of winding wheels. Another winding wheel has been set up near to the entrance of the museum. The museum has become an educational centre and provides information for schools on their visits.

The memorial to Woodhorn miners, killed in a colliery accident, has been re-erected at Woodhorn Mining Museum.

There is first a carpenter's shop in which traditional furniture is made, and visitors can see the work in progress. Then comes the entrance to the exhibition entitled "Gannin doon the Pit" and the visitor can get a good impression of what it was

like working in the mine, but without the danger, damp and dust. South East Northumberland once had 20 pits and now there is one. First is displayed the early history of mining and what it was like to work there, many workers being children before the mines reforms following the Commission Enquiry (1842) into child labour. Before this children of five years were employed as "trappers". The pits were ventilated by a fire drawing draught through the tunnels and the trap doors were to channel it. They had to be opened to let trolleys and baskets through. Mining equipment is shown, shovels, picks, drills and protective gear, and sound effects are provided, with voices in local dialect. There is a large mural design showing the local pits with shafts, tunnels and seams of coal – a geological survey. Then follows a specially attractive feature and perhaps most surprising – the Ashington Group of Pitmen Painters (1934-1986). Their work is now on permanent exhibition and a catalogue has been produced. The group started in 1934 as a Workers Association Class during a time of depression.

Robert Lyon from Kings College, Newcastle, was their tutor and splendid work was done. The paintings are in oil colours, particularly important at a drab time. Photographs of that time were almost entirely black and white. These paintings are in a light that never was there, like lights being switched on in a dark church. The pictures are a remarkable collection, especially good for the period 1934-1955, illustrating a chapter in social and industrial history. There is life in the streets, in the homes, on the allotments, with the pigeons and with the whippets. One shows a pug-mill and another the 'gin gang' on a farm. Similar apparatus was once used to raise coal from mines. To me the most surprising is the pit ponies having a bath. Of course they too got very dirty at their work! The other mining scenes below ground are very revealing.

Next in the museum are the larger pieces of equipment – tubs, stationary engines and a narrow gauge locomotive. Finally on the ground floor-is an exhibition of colliery railways with special reference to the neighbourhood. A video recording depicts the old trains taking miners to work and loading ships from Blyth staithes, at a time when many men were employed levelling the coal as deposited from the shutes in the holds of colliers.

Then passing the model of an office and a miner having a shower, the show goes upstairs with light from windows and a look over the landscape. Here is depicted what happened in the mining houses. Washday was all important with mother in a bad temper, resenting any interruptions. Hot water came from the set pot at one side of the fire. A pitman's wife could always have a good fire burning for boiling, baking, cooking and drying. Washing equipment is shown – the poss stick and the poss tub and the mangle. Roof water was collected in barrels for "soft" water. Hot water was also provided for the zinc bath which normally hung on an outside wall. There are models of mining people with recorded voices in dialect, telling what they were doing and about their lives. We get glimpses of life inside and outside; the leeks, the pigeons, the whippets, the allotments and the old bicycle, the common form of transport. So Woodhorn Museum can show us what it was like to live in a pit village.

Another building houses the Trade Union Exhibition, again illustrating an important part of miners' lives and work. A date chart depicts the development of Miners Unions in face of great difficulties. A special exhibition shows the life of one man who played an important part – Thomas Burt MP. Photographs of other miners and Labour Leaders are shown including Ebby Edwards. The obtaining of the vote in stages is shown. There is background music from Brass Bands and illustrations of Miners Picnics at Bedlington, Blyth and Morpeth. The Miners Banners, here on display, graced the proceedings. At one time there might be as many as 30 bands with banners competing with each other in the procession.

Walbottle Miners Banner depicts a pair of clasped hands, with the caption "Unity is Strength".

The banner of Ashington Miners Federation shows the pits of the group – Ellington, Woodhorn, Ashington, Linton and Lynemouth.

Sleekburn A banner shows the Houses of Parliament overlooking the Thames, which carries coal boats, showing the importance of coal in national history. West Sleekburn Miners Banner carries a portrait of Keir Hardie of Legbrannock, who was the first strictly "Labour" MP and shocked the establishment by appearing in the Commons with a red tie and cloth cap. The caption runs "His vision was our Inspiration". The Woodhorn branch NUM banner depicts "a century of coal". The colliery finally closed in 1981.

The pithead structures of Woodhorn Colliery remain standing as an important part of the Museum. The tall chimney was demolished.

Pictures are shown of other miners' activities, and in particular problems caused by strikes.

In other buildings to the north are the stables for the ponies, showing their harness and shoes, with the tools that were used to service them. The stables retain the authentic smell of horses. At the other end of the stable building is housed a smithy, which came from Falstone on the North Tyne. There are anvil and bellows and the various tools that the smith used. Collieries always had their blacksmiths, who dealt with all kinds of ironwork.

So altogether there is a comprehensive survey of mining life through the ages and the Museum is a monument to the industry.

WOODHORN

Woodhorn itself was a large ecclesiastic parish, which has been considerably reduced. Mackenzie in 1825 wrote of the village. "It contains a public house and a few cottages, inhabited by mechanics and husbandmen". The public house was called the "Plough" and there was no indication of mining. The name Woodhorn is of Anglo Saxon origin, meaning "woodcorner". Tomlinson (1888) wrote − "Woodhorn is a small village eight miles east by north of Morpeth, consisting of a few farms and cottages and an old windmill, which is a conspicuous landmark for sailors. Edward I was at Woodhorn on December 19th 1292".

It is recorded that in the 8th century King Ceolwulf granted land here to the monks of Lindisfarne when he became a member of the community. The first church was probably built of timber, since there were plenty of trees locally.

A number of carved Anglo Saxon stones have been recovered from the site, which show its antiquity. The present church, dedicated to St Mary, consists of a strong squarish west tower, a nave with aisles and a long chancel. It was very much restored in 1843, when the fabric was in bad condition. New Norman type windows were put in and the upper part of the tower was restored. Despite what Pevsner says, the tower is buttressed and carries a newel stair in the south-east corner. The stonework shows discoloration from smoking chimneys and the railway that passes near. The old coal locomotives blew out clouds of black smoke. The burn that passes by the church is fitful, but once it powered a watermill. There would be a reservoir for the water, which has now dried up and the ruined walls of the mill buildings can be detected in the field below the church. Some of the stones have been transferred to the churchyard walls. Stone originally came from the quarries near the windmill, which is now a shell without sails or machinery. It still remains a landmark, though overshadowed by the chimneys of Alcan. Might not Alcan provide aluminium sails for the mill and use it as a source of energy, which would be friendly to the environment?

Woodhorn had belonged to the Widdrington family, whose estates were forfeited in the Jacobite rebellions. Their successors were the Waddiloves, who acquired most of the Woodhorn land and became Lords of the Manor. The moor was enclosed and there were seven farms. The largest was the Manor Farm, which was

CHAPTER XII: NEWBIGGIN

John Wallis in 1769 wrote – "Newbiggin, a marine villa, inhabited chiefly by fishermen, consisting of one long irregular street: several granaries in it for export from one of the finest bays before it on the coast of this county, formed by two promontories of freestone rocks, spacious, the bottom of sand: corn ships of about 60 tons burthen, coming up to the town: larger ships father in riding, in 5, 6 or 7 fathom of water in security from tempests from the north and north east. On the northern point of the bay is the vestiges of an old pier: many of the stones and some of the piles of wood conspicuous in low water.

On the NE side of the harbour is the church dedicated to St Bartholomew: the middle aisle and the spire only now remaining: a small gallery to the west end: at the east end, above the altar table is the King's Arms, cut in wood in high relief said to have been the stern of a ship cast away in a storm upon the rocks: one bell in the spire: the churchyard small: a delightful prospect from it. On the north side of it about 100 yards from the sea banks in the cavity of a rock is a fresh water spring, called St Mary's Well, accessible only at ebb tides". (Wallis)

Hodgson mentions "a large portion of it (Newbiggin) consists of an unenclosed tract called the Links or Newbigging Moor, on which the proprietors of the other part of the chapelry have cattle stints in various proportions. An unsightly and profitless marsh called the Carr, which is formed by the little brook which comes past Woodhorn and a stream from the north overflowing it, runs along the south side of the Moor and stands in need of improvement".

In 1821 Newbiggin contained 82 houses and 434 people, mostly fisherfolk "a fine race of people, whose occupation makes them intrepid, but subjects them to perils that often bereave their families of their support". (Hodgson)

He described and sketched the chapel, which was much neglected, but the tower, built of good masonry and in a graceful form, was a well-known landmark for shipping. The nave 75 feet by 16 feet once had aisles to north and south. But these had been demolished and the masonry of the outer walls was used to fill the arches, which were still visible on the exterior of the church. The chancel which was 50 feet long was roofless, but nevertheless appeared to have the attraction of a folly. It had a very impressive east window comprised of five long lights.

"Here are no inscriptions, monuments or carvings, worthy of notice excepting certain crosses engraven on marbles in the floor of the nave and on ancient gravestones, built up in the walls of the church or scattered over the churchyard." Hodgson went on to say that it "was to me a favourite spot: and the fine sands of the bay, the long dry moor and its bold and rocky shores, can never fail to be interesting resorts to any that can be gratified with surveying the vastness and admiring the power and productions of the mighty deep". He had a great interest in geology, seaweeds and fish.

A visitation to the chapel in 1826 by Archdeacon Singleton reported that rents and dues to the church were not properly paid and that the chancel was being used

that might date to the late Saxon period just before the Conquest. It has been suggested that the early stone church might date to this period. A carved stone shows the crucifixion with Christ between two figures, St Mary and St John. It is carved as if it were a window, and it is not clear what its purpose was; perhaps the panel of an Easter Sepulchre or a 13th century tomb. There are also a number of medieval recumbent slabs, decorated with crosses and some church furnishings. All of these are permanent and extra to the periodic varied exhibitions.

Demonstrations of particular arts and crafts are given from time to time, and a number of items on display are for sale. Exhibitions may well be accompanied with pleasant music, and at times concerts are held here. So Woodhorn Church Museum is well worth visiting for its artistic and cultural merits, in contrast to the more utilitarian Colliery Museum, but both reflect the life of the neighbourhood. We now move to what was part of Woodhorn parish, but has now taken over and provides the church for services – namely Newbiggin-by-the-Sea.

Views across the bay to Newbiggin Church.

rented by the Wilson family. Joseph and his son Jacob gained reputations as farmers. Jacob went to Cirencester Agricultural College and became an expert on farm machinery. His expertise extended to all branches of farming, and he was frequently asked for advice. He helped the Northumberland Agricultural Society and worked for the Royal Agricultural Show. In 1889 he received a knighthood from Queen Victoria and was agent for several Northumberland estates.

An aerial view of Woodhorn before the Alcan alterations; showing Manor Farm and Mill. (© University of Newcastle upon Tyne).

When I first saw Woodhorn Manor it must have been one of the finest farmsteads in Northumberland. There was a grand stone house and a range of buildings that could have been easily converted to houses. The buildings had quality and a steam engine with a tall chimney had provided power for a full range of machinery for threshing and grinding and which were still there. A copper lined silo underground was the receptacle for grain. The buildings, however, were demolished before the Alcan development, when buildings were erected to the north of the village. The blacksmith in the cottage opposite was Mr Pyle, whose family had been there for more than a century. Henry Pyle was there in 1855 and Richard Hindhaugh was the miller. The wind and water mills worked to complement each other, since neither wind or water would be in continuous supply.

The large parish of Woodhorn in 1855 included Cresswell, Ellington, Hirst, Lynemouth, Newbiggin and North Seaton. In 1888 North Seaton had a population of 1,846, Newbiggin 1,388 while Woodhorn had only 177. Cresswell, Ellington,

Hirst and Lynemouth in time were lost. In modern times it became impossible to maintain Woodhorn Church, and in 1972 the title of parish church was transferred to that of St Bartholomew at Newbiggin. Fortunately Woodhorn Church was saved by Wansbeck District Council for use as a museum and exhibition centre which has become a great attraction. The graveyard contains a collection of memorial stones that might well be recorded for historical interest. Built into the walls of the church are medieval monumental stones and a sculptured figure on the west wall of the tower. Pevsner comments on the church – "Externally not promising... but inside very much worthwhile". The porch contains some medieval carved stones, parts of grave covers with floriated crosses. On entering the church the light colour of the walls shows up features to great effect and the Victorian glass windows glow with colour – not the highest class but very attractive. Then there are the pillars – the first near the door has been exposed to its base, showing that it was set upon the outside wall of the early Norman church. The arch connects with this same wall at the south-west angle of the nave. The arches were introduced when the aisles were added and the church extended. Dowsing, followed by excavation, shows that the early stone church had an apsidal east end, which is marked on the floor of a much extended chancel. Other early features to be noticed are the narrow windows above the arches. The one in the north aisle is complete. It has a long narrow arched opening to the outside and a very wide splay, admitting much more light than might be expected. The south window loses some of its length since here the arches are higher. The arches adjacent to the chancel are double width, indicating that at one time the church had transepts. The large pillars on the north side have carved capitals. The arches above the capitals and pillars have been cut out of the original wall, since the thickness of the wall above is the same as the bases of the pillars. The south aisle pillars are plain and the arches single stepped. The tower arch is also single stepped. Off one corner is the narrow newel stair leading to the top of the tower. It can be detected from the outside by small narrow windows. The chancel arch is 13th century – double chamfered with shafts resting on corbels. The north one has carved leaves and a finely carved human head. The chancel is now used to exhibit Anglo Saxon and medieval carved stones. There are two medieval bells on display – the treble bell is dated 1250-90 and the other was cast in the 14th century.

Near the bells is the best monument in the church – the effigy of Dame Agnes de Valance, wife of High Balliol, brother of Edward Balliol, made King of Scotland by Edward I. The figure of the lady, sometimes called an abbess, is a relief carving, showing her beneath a canopy under which is a seated figure of the Virgin Mary with two worshippers. Four mourners attend at the head and feet of the lady.

On the other side of the chancel is displayed a collection of carved stones and figures. The largest is a broken medieval slab from the graveyard of old Hepple chapel. An inscription in Latin translated runs – "Here lies the Lady Marjorie, wife of Lord Robert Tailbois." She was probably buried towards the end of the reign of Henry III, c1266. There are remains of an Anglican cross with interlacing patterns

Hirst and Lynemouth in time were lost. In modern times it became impossible to maintain Woodhorn Church, and in 1972 the title of parish church was transferred to that of St Bartholomew at Newbiggin. Fortunately Woodhorn Church was saved by Wansbeck District Council for use as a museum and exhibition centre which has become a great attraction. The graveyard contains a collection of memorial stones that might well be recorded for historical interest. Built into the walls of the church are medieval monumental stones and a sculptured figure on the west wall of the tower. Pevsner comments on the church – "Externally not promising... but inside very much worthwhile". The porch contains some medieval carved stones, parts of grave covers with floriated crosses. On entering the church the light colour of the walls shows up features to great effect and the Victorian glass windows glow with colour – not the highest class but very attractive. Then there are the pillars – the first near the door has been exposed to its base, showing that it was set upon the outside wall of the early Norman church. The arch connects with this same wall at the south-west angle of the nave. The arches were introduced when the aisles were added and the church extended. Dowsing, followed by excavation, shows that the early stone church had an apsidal east end, which is marked on the floor of a much extended chancel. Other early features to be noticed are the narrow windows above the arches. The one in the north aisle is complete. It has a long narrow arched opening to the outside and a very wide splay, admitting much more light than might be expected. The south window loses some of its length since here the arches are higher. The arches adjacent to the chancel are double width, indicating that at one time the church had transepts. The large pillars on the north side have carved capitals. The arches above the capitals and pillars have been cut out of the original wall, since the thickness of the wall above is the same as the bases of the pillars. The south aisle pillars are plain and the arches single stepped. The tower arch is also single stepped. Off one corner is the narrow newel stair leading to the top of the tower. It can be detected from the outside by small narrowwindows. The chancel arch is 13th century – double chamfered with shafts resting on corbels.. The north one has carved leaves and a finely carved human head. The chancel is now used to exhibit Anglo Saxon and medieval carved stones. There are two medieval bells on display – the treble bell is dated 1250-90 and the other was cast in the 14th century.

Near the bells is the best monument in the church – the effigy of Dame Agnes de Valance, wife of High Balliol, brother of Edward Balliol, made King of Scotland by Edward I. The figure of the lady, sometimes called an abbess, is a relief carving, showing her beneath a canopy under which is a seated figure of the Virgin Mary with two worshippers. Four mourners attend at the head and feet of the lady.

On the other side of the chancel is displayed a collection of carved stones and figures. The largest is a broken medieval slab from the graveyard of old Hepple chapel. An inscription in Latin translated runs – "Here lies the Lady Marjorie, wife of Lord Robert Tailbois." She was probably buried towards the end of the reign of Henry III, c1266. There are remains of an Anglican cross with interlacing patterns

that might date to the late Saxon period just before the Conquest. It has been suggested that the early stone church might date to this period. A carved stone shows the crucifixion with Christ between two figures, St Mary and St John. It is carved as if it were a window, and it is not clear what its purpose was; perhaps the panel of an Easter Sepulchre or a 13th century tomb. There are also a number of medieval recumbent slabs, decorated with crosses and some church furnishings. All of these are permanent and extra to the periodic varied exhibitions.

Demonstrations of particular arts and crafts are given from time to time, and a number of items on display are for sale. Exhibitions may well be accompanied with pleasant music, and at times concerts are held here. So Woodhorn Church Museum is well worth visiting for its artistic and cultural merits, in contrast to the more utilitarian Colliery Museum, but both reflect the life of the neighbourhood. We now move to what was part of Woodhorn parish, but has now taken over and provides the church for services – namely Newbiggin-by-the-Sea.

Views across the bay to Newbiggin Church.

118

CHAPTER XII: NEWBIGGIN

John Wallis in 1769 wrote – "Newbiggin, a marine villa, inhabited chiefly by fishermen, consisting of one long irregular street: several granaries in it for export from one of the finest bays before it on the coast of this county, formed by two promontories of freestone rocks, spacious, the bottom of sand: corn ships of about 60 tons burthen, coming up to the town: larger ships father in riding, in 5, 6 or 7 fathom of water in security from tempests from the north and north east. On the northern point of the bay is the vestiges of an old pier: many of the stones and some of the piles of wood conspicuous in low water.

On the NE side of the harbour is the church dedicated to St Bartholomew: the middle aisle and the spire only now remaining: a small gallery to the west end: at the east end, above the altar table is the King's Arms, cut in wood in high relief said to have been the stern of a ship cast away in a storm upon the rocks: one bell in the spire: the churchyard small: a delightful prospect from it. On the north side of it about 100 yards from the sea banks in the cavity of a rock is a fresh water spring, called St Mary's Well, accessible only at ebb tides". (Wallis)

Hodgson mentions "a large portion of it (Newbiggin) consists of an unenclosed tract called the Links or Newbigging Moor, on which the proprietors of the other part of the chapelry have cattle stints in various proportions. An unsightly and profitless marsh called the Carr, which is formed by the little brook which comes past Woodhorn and a stream from the north overflowing it, runs along the south side of the Moor and stands in need of improvement".

In 1821 Newbiggin contained 82 houses and 434 people, mostly fisherfolk "a fine race of people, whose occupation makes them intrepid, but subjects them to perils that often bereave their families of their support". (Hodgson)

He described and sketched the chapel, which was much neglected, but the tower, built of good masonry and in a graceful form, was a well-known landmark for shipping. The nave 75 feet by 16 feet once had aisles to north and south. But these had been demolished and the masonry of the outer walls was used to fill the arches, which were still visible on the exterior of the church. The chancel which was 50 feet long was roofless, but nevertheless appeared to have the attraction of a folly. It had a very impressive east window comprised of five long lights.

"Here are no inscriptions, monuments or carvings, worthy of notice excepting certain crosses engraven on marbles in the floor of the nave and on ancient gravestones, built up in the walls of the church or scattered over the churchyard." Hodgson went on to say that it "was to me a favourite spot: and the fine sands of the bay, the long dry moor and its bold and rocky shores, can never fail to be interesting resorts to any that can be gratified with surveying the vastness and admiring the power and productions of the mighty deep". He had a great interest in geology, seaweeds and fish.

A visitation to the chapel in 1826 by Archdeacon Singleton reported that rents and dues to the church were not properly paid and that the chancel was being used

a burial place on the plea that this part of the building was never completed. Other reports indicate that the graveyard suffered severely from erosion, with skulls and bones being scattered by the pounding waves. "The old picturesque church of St Bartholomew is situated on a point of land projecting into the sea, the spray of angry waves reaching into the churchyard and washing the graves".

Another element is the shifting sands and after a gale and high tide the graves and the surrounding areas can be covered deep in sand. Gravestones suffer from erosion and some of them have been worn through.

The fishing community at Newbiggin had been under obligations to the church from medieval times and tithes continued to be collected. A tithe of £2 had to be paid on each boat plus a tithe on all lobsters landed. In 1771 there was a fishermen's rebellion and they refused to pay these tithes. The Rector replied by refusing to continue services in the chapel – he lived at Woodhorn Rectory. This explains why the chapel of St Bartholomew fell into such disrepair. In 1845, however, Rev. J R Shipperstone decided that the chapel should be restored and, with the help of the community, this came about and services were resumed. The main fabric of the church was restored. The chancel was rebuilt and roofed. A number of old medieval sepulchral stones, adorned with floriated crosses, were built into the inside of the walls, where they appear rather attractive. Some medieval carved human heads have also been found places – two at the porch entrance. The aisles were not restored and so the outer walls still contain the pillars and arches of the former aisled church. The tower, were it not for the medieval spire, might appear as Anglo Saxon, since it is comparatively slender. So it was pleasing to all that the chapel was restored, especially since during the second part of the 19th century Newbiggin attracted more and more visitors – some for lengthy holidays and some for days only. It was damaged by mines in the last war.

THE FISHING INDUSTRY

Fishing expanded enormously between about 1851 and 1914 with a growing population and improvements in transport. The herring boom in particular increased employment since in addition to the fishermen, coopers were required to make barrels. Curers and female gutters and packers were also needed. Fisher girls followed the fleet as the shoals of herring moved. Newbiggin provided a place for smoking and coopering, serving ships that were not based on the local port. In 1862, 142 cobles were registered at Newbiggin. Each fisherman might have several for different types of fishing – line fishing, drift net and herring drift net fishing. From 1870 the larger cobles were replaced by "Mules" and from 1876 larger Scottish designed and built boats were used in herring fishing. These were crewed by six to eight men, and herring could be taken 20 to 40 miles out at sea. The smaller cobles were served by three men and a boy. The herring season was from late July for six weeks, and boats might travel from Eyemouth to Lowestoft, calling at different ports on the way. When the boats were not in use, they were laid up at the mouth of the Wansbeck. The total number of keep boats owned and operated from Newbiggin at this time was 58.

Line fishing from Newbiggin was for white fish. Baiting the lines with mussels or limpets was a time consuming process involving the whole family. Both had to be gathered, skinned and hooked. Nets were used for taking salmon and sea trout. These also had to be mended and maintained. Other problems were providing sand bags for ballast, carrying boxes or baskets for the fish. Women played an important part in this as they did for launching and hauling in the boats. In their spare time, waiting for the return of boats, they would be occupied in knitting the traditional woollen ware for fishermen the ganseys, knitted on four pins with no seams (the garment of Jesus Christ, fisherman, was seamless).

Women worked in the preparation and sale of fish. It was carried in creels and sold in local streets or further afield. Fisher wives could travel a considerable distance with their fish, but seemingly they were not very welcome on trains or buses!

THE COAL INDUSTRY

When Newbiggin Colliery was sunk, a mining community developed in the neighbourhood, very distinct from the fishermen who were said to be hostile. Waste from the mines had to be continually dumped in the sea and this is not to the liking of fish or fishermen.

From this has developed yet another type of community, still very active the seacoalers. With the coming and ebbing of the tide there appears on the bright sandy beaches what seem to be giant black eyebrows. These are deposits of sea coal, usually very small, but there can be bigger lumps. Sea-coalers arrive and sacks are loaded up and pushed away. Some may arrive with ponies and carts. The ponies are usually piebald and attractive. At times I have met a pony taking a walk or trot through the streets on its own and they stray over the golf course on Newbiggin Moor. Sea-coaling still goes on and other vehicles are used. There is a road down past the entrance to the golf course, which leads to a dump of black sand and sea coal. I have read "The Newbiggin freeholders rights to back to 1235 and include rights of the foreshore so that they can stop people gathering sea coal." (Parson) Has this right fallen out of use? Newbiggin, which means "new building" and implies a new medieval settlement by the sea was a very important place in medieval times. It belonged to the Barony of Balliol and the lord had the right of a "gallows" to punish offenders.

MEDIEVAL NEWBIGGIN

By the 13th century Newbiggin had achieved borough status like Morpeth. It had a market on Mondays and an annual fair from 23-25 August. In the Lay Subsidy Roll of 1296, compiled for taxation purposes by officials of Edward I, it is shown to be one of the most populous and wealthy places in the county. Thirty-six taxpayers were assessed as £43:6s:4d and 12 jurors at £54:13s:7d – twice the amount of Morpeth. Only Newcastle and Corbridge were rated more highly. Morpeth and Newbiggin each paid 6s towards the expenses of Knights of the Shire (ie Members of Parliament). Newbiggin was a fishing community at a time when

fish and ships were of the greatest importance. Fish was for the feeding of all, but especially the religious of the monasteries. Fish could be preserved by salt or smoking and could be exported.

Newbiggin was very much in use during the Scottish Wars of the three Edwards. Edward I in 1292 at Norham chose John Balliol as King of Scotland, but later made war on him. Both Edward I and Edward II required ships from Newbiggin. Edward II granted a toll on merchandise using the port, so that improvements could be made to the quay. In 1352 Bishop Hatfield of Durham granted indulgences (pardons for sins) to those who contributed to the cost of a breakwater. The furious seas through the centuries attacked the port and eroded the cliffs, so that only the remains of the breakwater and quay were visible in Hodgson's time.

The importance of the port accounts for the size of the earlier Church, which with its tower was a well known navigation landmark. "The spire is a mark to sea-men, of great use to ships coming from the North and Baltic Seas as a direction for their southward course." (Hodgson)

NEWBIGGIN FREEHOLDERS

The freeholders of Newbiggin like those of Morpeth had houses in the town with property attached, but they also had stints or shares of the Town Moor, providing them with land for grazing or crops. Freeholders were involved in local government and also took part in elections. In 1296 48 taxpayers were named and in 1888 "To the east of the village is Newbiggin Moor, or Common, about 2 miles in length and containing 232 acres. It is the property of the freeholders (at present 46), who have exercised rights and privileges since AD 1235. It is a great resort for lovers of bowling and golfing, and for the latter game it is said to be the best ground in Great Britain". (Bulmer)

The freeholders of Newbiggin still function. The freeholds of the Moor have been detached in some cases from the houses in the village. The freeholders may live in other parts of the country or abroad. On the day of the Beating of the Bounds in May, they meet in some hostelry, formerly the Old Ship to discuss business. Then they beat the bounds mainly on foot, but there are horseriders. Nuts are thrown to the bystanders. If there is the ceremony of initiation for a new freeholder, he is taken to the "dunting" stone in the middle of the moor. Then existing freeholders take him by feet and shoulders and bump him on the stone. (The original has been replaced by a chunk of concrete.) Words are spoken over him and he becomes a freeholder. After the ceremony the freeholders and invited visitors retire to the hostelry for a dinner and speeches. In such a way the customs of Newbiggin are still alive.

There are no actual divisions of the Moor, so this is why it can still be used as a Golf Course. There are 80 stints in all, and in the past a stint or part of a stint would allow the grazing of a certain number of animals. The number varied for horses or cattle or sheep; sheep being the largest number allowed. A freeholder

might have part of a stint, a stint or several stints. The freeholders hold their own "court" to settle matters of business between themselves. At Newbiggin they and not the local council still own the land. They have resisted any such take-over, whereas the Town Moor at Newcastle and Common at Morpeth were taken over by the respective councils. So the freeholders of Newbiggin are a community that has continued unbroken for more than 750 years, and may they long survive in a world where greater authorities try to engulf the smaller, just as the sea continually threatens and erodes their land. Defences have been erected against the sea and may rights to the land be similarly defended.

The picture of Newbiggin in 1881 shows that there were 1,388 inhabitants and 19 lodging house keepers. Accommodation was provided at seven hotels and inns; three beer houses and four refreshment rooms competed for custom. Ten Grocers and Provision Dealers included the local Co-operative Society. There were two fish merchants and six fishmongers, six tailors and six cowkeepers, five bakers and five butchers. The railway had arrived in 1872 to facilitate the coming of visitors and the travel of local people. "The village, which is situated by the seashore is chiefly inhabited by fishermen and is a favourite bathing resort, during summer months. There is a fine stretch of sandy beach extending nearly a mile in length and a considerable distance seawards, where the little ones may gather "sheels of ocean", whilst their seniors are enjoying the luxury of a sea bath in comparative safety. There are bathing machines for the use of the ladies". (Bulmer)

The Old Ship Inn had special indoor baths of the spa type and billiards were also available. People of importance, like Sir Charles Middleton of Belsay, had houses and property here.

The Newbiggin Golf Club had its headquarters at the Old Ship Inn. The President was Sir Matthew White Ridley, but there was a Working Mens Golf Club held at the Coble Inn. Andrew Elliott was a greyhound trainer and John Lisle Dawson, pleasure boat proprietor, which shows that there was more to the sea than fishing. John Dawson was a shipowner and freeholder. Some persons had multiple occupations. Robert Watson was manager of the gas works, plumber and golf club and ball maker, living at Paragon cottage. Thomas Wilkie was a draper, freeholder and secretary to the Newbiggin Freeholders. He was also agent for the Royal Fire and Life Insurance Company. John Peel, no bobby or hunter, was collector of rates and inspector of nuisance.

"Newbiggin has been greatly improved in recent years by the erection of superior houses for the accommodation of visitors. A gas company was formed in 1865 and the necessary works were erected, but the village is still dependent on pumps for its water supply. Fishing is now its only trade. Haddock, cod, ling, whiting, also crabs and lobsters are plentiful and a few salmon trout & herring are taken in their respective seasons. The first lifeboat in connection with the Royal National Lifeboat Institution was placed here in 1852 & since that time there have been 210 lives saved & timely assistance rendered to boats in distress". (Bulmer)

The railway helped the development of Newbiggin, since business men who

wanted to live here could commute to Newcastle and Tyneside. Also about this time the Morpeth Herald would report persons who were on holiday at Newbiggin. The railway also provided cheap day excursions to the sea and the beach could be crowded. Some of these visitors behaved in such a way as not to enhance the reputation of the resort. Between 1891 and 1911 the population increased from 1,388 to 3,446 and although improvements took place in housing there was still a shortage of shelter and some people lived in shacks or overturned boats on the beach.

A very important development was the sinking of a colliery shaft on the "Carrs" to the north of the village in 1908; and three years later large quantities of coal were being mined. It meant industry close at hand and more housing for mines. The pit was sunk on freehold land belonging to Mr Sidney of Cowpen Hall who had purchased several stints. After a legal battle with Mr Waddilove, Lord of the Manor, and the Freeholders Mr Sidney's company secured the right to mine under the moor. The Freeholders were paid money, but their land suffered. The golf course in particular became less attractive, since the surface and atmosphere deteriorated. Mining here and further up the coast caused considerable subsidence and increased the devastating effects of the storms. Colliery waste was wantonly tipped into the waters and Lynemouth had an aerial ropeway for tipping directly into the sea. Some of the rubbish returned as sea coal, and the beach suffered pollution since household rubbish and rubbish from the boats was thrown into the waters. The fishermen resented this pollution and some visitors stayed away. In 1897 the description was – "A beautiful bay on the German Ocean, its sands being remarkably smooth, firm and safe. It has become a favourite watering place and is much frequented in summer months". (Morpeth Herald)

This picture was to fade fairly rapidly, coal extraction and tipping of waste being the main factors.

The construction of a promenade in 1924 failed to halt the advance of the sea and property was damaged. The freeholders lost acres of lands to coal mining and the tides. The cobles continued to be employed in fishing. A coble was a very strongly built boat, with a flat bottom, responding well to oars and sail. Until after 1900 sails were used, each boat having a main sail and two masts. The longer mast was used in fine weather and the shorter in bad conditions. From 1919 the boats were powered by engines and after World War II tractors were used for haulage to and from the beach. The coble was moved on a pair of wheels to or from the sea. A naval historian has written – "The coble is considered one of the best in the world for coming through breaking waves on to the beach. The size and power of the cobles working off Newbiggin beach earned them particularly high regard". (Simper)

Today some ten boats can be seen grounded near the Lifeboat Station or at other times returning with a catch to the harbour. The women are no longer needed to haul in. A tractor backs the pair of wheels into the shallow water and under the coble. It is hauled out sometimes with difficulty, when a second tractor is attached. So the struggle against the sea goes on.

Cobles at rest above the grasp of the tide at Newbiggin.

The colliery has gone and housing has extended northwards on Woodhorn Demesne. The golfers play now under the shadows of Alcan, its power station fuelled with Ellington coal. There is still a variety of shops, but the supermarket has arrived. Newbiggin has a modern Community and Leisure Centre.

The impact of visitors today is shown by the development of Caravan Parks. There is a large one at Church Point, where the full effect of sea breezes can be felt. A larger, but less obtrusive site is at Sandy Bay at the mouth of the Wansbeck, where ships were able to take refuge and cobles could be laid up. There are interesting walks along the coast between the two sites, including the promenade which has been rebuilt at considerable cost. The process of protection against erosion is still continuing.

Along the main street the names of the old hostelries remain – the Railway, The New Dolphin (restored in 1908), the Queen's Head, the Queen Victoria and The Old Ship. All are reminders of the last century and last in line at the end of the road is the Cresswell Arms, "the last pub before Norway". Strictly speaking refreshment can be obtained nearer the sea at the bar of the Golf Club, which has one of the stints and where the Freeholders met in May 1992.

Northwards loom the Alcan Works and beneath the beach, the eroded cliff and the activities of the sea-coalers. On the turf the golfers are putting and an occasional horse appears. Southwards rises the Church and the curve of Newbiggin harbour with promenade, sea wall and houses. Beyond another jutting headland is a final

view of the mouth of the Wansbeck, which has again altered course. Then appear industrial activities of North Blyth, cranes, the Alcan Terminal and the harbour mouth. Further still the coast curves to Tynemouth, whence ships may emerge less frequently, but much larger in size. Along Blyth pier the sails of windmills are turning to make electricity. Out to sea we are reminded of–

The Odyssey – Andrew Lang

"As such an one were glad to know the brine
Salt on his lips and the large air again
So gladly from the songs of modern speech
Men turn and see the stars and feel the free
Shrill wind beyond the close of heavy flowers
And through the music of the languid hours
They hear like Ocean on a western beach,
The surge and thunder of the Odyssey".

The rocky headland at Newbiggin that is constantly battered by the waves.

GLOSSARY

advowson: patronage, right to present to a benefice (church living)

apse: semicircular recess at the end of a church

barmkin: the enclosure connected with a castle, also called pale or pele

bellcote: belfry in the form of a small gabled or roofed housing for bells

castellated: adorned with battlements like a castle

chamfered: channelled/fluted

clerestory: the upper storey of a church, usually nave, furnished with windows, hence "clearstory"

corbel: projecting stone to carry a beam

cupola: dome

fenestration: the arrangement, mode of design of windows

floriated: adorned by floral elements or designs

mudyllyons: medallions – decorative panels or tablets

mullions: the upright divisions of the lights of a window, horizontal or cross divisions by transoms

multivallate: having several ramparts or lines of defence

newel: upright column round which winds a circular stair

pilasters: representation of columns in flat relief as ornamentation to a wall

quatrefoil: fourleaf

reredos: painted or carved screen behind and above an altar

sacristy: a room in a church for sacred vessels and vestments

sedilia: seats for priests (usually three) on the south side of the chancel of a church

sheilings: temporary dwellings used by shepherds living on summer pastures

spandrels: spaces between adjacent arches

trefoil headed: three leaf, three lobes in a shape for tracery

BIBLIOGRAPHY

Allsopp, B & Clarke, U	Historic Architecture of Northumberland and Newcastle upon Tyne. Oriel Press, 1977.
	Archaeologia Aeliana or Miscellaneous Tracts Relating to Antiquity. The Society of Antiquaries of Newcastle upon Tyne, 1857.
Armstrong, A	Map of Northumberland. 1769.
Armstrong, C	Pilgrimage from Nenthead. Methuen, 1938.
Bates, C J	The Border Holds of Northumberland. Society of Antiquaries of Newcastle upon Tyne, 1891.
Bibby, R	Bothal Observed. Graham, 1973.
Bogg, E	A Thousand Miles of Wandering in the Border Country, Lakeland and Ribblesdale. Mawson Swan & Morgan, 1898.
Bosanquet, R E	In the Troublesome Times. Spredden Press, 1989.
Bulmer, T F	History, Topography and Directory of Northumberland. 1888.
Burt, T	Thomas Burt – MP, pitman and privy councillor: an autobiography. T Fisher Unwin Ltd, 1924.
Coatsworth, E	The Carved Stones of Woodhorn Church. Wansbeck District Council, 1981.
	Domesday Book 35, Supplementary Volume Boldon book. Phillimore, 1982.
Fergusson, J	Mitford Church (St Mary Magdalene): its history, restoration and associations. 1884.
	Morpeth: the official guide of the Morpeth Corporation. 1906.
	Morpeth from the accession to the jubilee of Queen Victoria (1837-1887). 1887.
Fraser, C & Emsley, K	Northumbria. Batsford, 1978.
Graham, P A	Highways and Byways in Northumbria. Macmillan, 1920.
Griffin, A R	The Collier. Shire Publications, 1982.

Harrison, Bill	Ashington: a history in photographs. Northumberland County Library, 1990.
Hepple, L W	A History of Northumberland and Newcastle upon Tyne. Phillimore, 1976.
Hinde, T	Capability Brown: The story of a master gardener. Hutchinson, 1986.
Hodgson, J	History of Northumberland Pt 2, Vols 1 & 2. The author, 1832.
Hutchinson, W	A View of Northumberland with an Excursion to the Abbey of Montrose in Scotland. 1776.
McCord, N	North East History From the Air. Phillimore, 1991.
McGuinness, P	An Outline History of Woodhorn. Wansbeck District Council, 1986.
MacKenzie, A	An Historical, Topographical and Descriptive View of the County of Northumberland. 1825.
Martin, S B	Bedlington. The author, 1986.
	Bomarsund and Stakeford. The author, 1985.
	Choppington township. The author, 1983.
	Netherton (Nedderton). The author, 1987.
	Sleekburn (The Station), with Bank Top, East Sleekburn and Red Row. The author, 1985.
	West Sleekburn (The Winnin). The author, 1984.
Moffatt, F C	Another Penn'orth of Herrin'. The author, 1985.
	Border cavalcade – life a century ago. The author, 1989.
	Morpeth (between the wars) 3 Vols. The author, 1980.
	100 Years On: Morpeth Conservative Club centenary 1887-1987. The author, 1988.
	Morpeth: faces and places of old. The author, 1987.
	Morpeth Golf Club 1906-81. The author, 1981.
	Morpeth: a thumbnail look for visitors. The author. (n.d.)
	Pictorial Morpeth: new vistas. The author, 1984.
	A Tap at the End of the Raa. The author, 1990.

	Turnpike Road to Tartan Track. The author, 1979.
	Two Penn'orth of Herrin'. The author, 1982.
Monthly Chronicle	
Morpeth Herald	
Morris, J E	Northumberland. Methuen, 1916.
	Northumberland (Arthur Mee Series) C L S Linnell ed. Hodder, 1964.
Ogle, (Sir) Henry	Ogles of Bothal. 1902.
National Trust	National Trust Guide Cape 1984
Parson, W & White, W	History directory and gazetteer of Durham and Northumberland and the towns and counties of Newcastle-upon-Tyne and Berwick-upon-Tweed, 1827.
Pevsner, N	Northumberland, with notes on the Roman antiquities. Penguin, 1957.
Robinson, J	Newbiggin-by-the-Sea: a fishing community. Northumberland County Library, 1991.
Robson, R A	The Urban District of Ashington, Northumberland. Ashington UDC, 1966.
Rowland, T H	Visit Historic Morpeth. The author, 1987.
	Bygone Morpeth. Phillimore, 1989.
	Medieval Castles, Towers, Peles and Bastles of Northumberland. The author, 1987.
	Discovering Northumberland: a handbook of local history. The author, 1973.
Sharp, T	Northumberland. Faber & Faber, 1939.
Simper, R	Britain's Maritime Heritage. David & Charles, 1982.
Stroud, D	Capability Brown. Faber, 1984.
Tomlinson, W W	Comprehensive guide to the county of Northumberland. Davis Books, 1985.
Trevelyan, (Sir) Charles	Wallington: its history and treasures. The author, 1947.
Turner, W C	A New Herball. Carcanet, 1989.

Tweddle, A H	Town trails for Morpethians 1-9. The author, 1987-90.
Wallace, J	The history of Blyth from the Norman Conquest to the present day. John Robinson, 1962.
Wallis, J	The natural history and antiquities of Northumberland and of so much of Durham as lies between the Rivers Tyne and Tweed commonly called the North Bishopric. 1769.
White, W	Northumberland and the Border. Chapman Hall, 1859.
Wilson, F R	An architectural survey of the churches in the Archdeaconry of Lindisfarne in the County of Northumberland. 1870.
Wood, G B	North Country Profile. Robert Hale, 1973.

ADDITIONAL SOURCES

Newbiggin Freemen	Records and Information
Local District Council Guides	
Parish Registers	Bothal, Hartburn, Kirkwhelpington, Mitford, Morpeth and Woodhorn

Oral information from many individuals in particular places

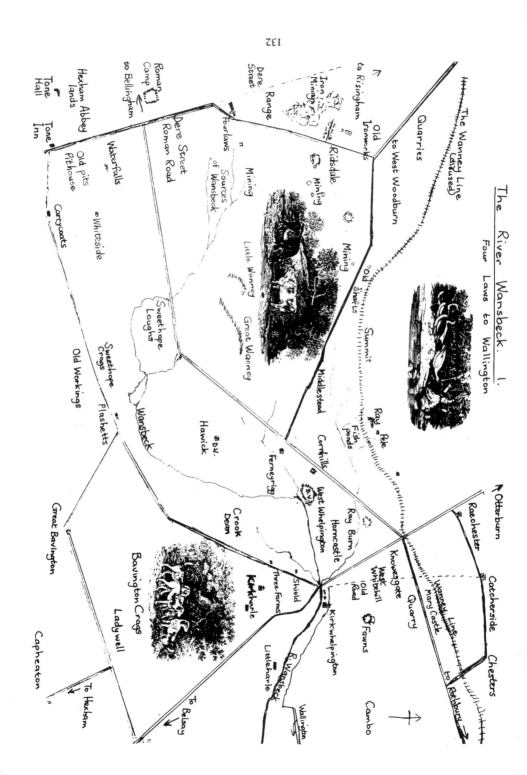

The River Wansbeck. I.

Four Laws to Wallington.

Forest burn Gate

Kilns
Viaduct

FONTBURN
RESERVOIR

R. Font

Nunnykirk
Hall

Folly House

to Wingates

Ewesley

Coal houses

Beacon
Hill

Rothley Lakes

Witton Shields

Stanton

Folly

Netherwitton

Rothley Cross Roads

Shelly

R. Font

Benridge

Gallows
Hill

Folly

Rothley
Crag

Longwitton

Kilns

Thornton Moor

Longshaws

Hartington

R. Hart

Nunriding
Hall

Cambo

Hartburn

Meldon Park

Mitford

Wallington

Marlish

R. Hart

Middleton

Angerton Hall

Meg's Bridge

Wallington Bridge

R. Wansbeck

Low
Angerton

Rivergreen

Meldon

Penny Hill

Bolam   Hall   Church

Kirkharle

Gallowhill

Shortflatt

Whalton

Harnham

to Hexham   Capheaton

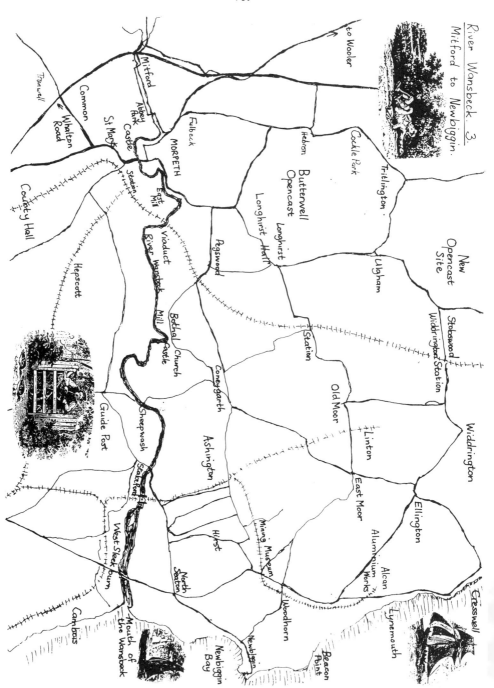

River Wansbeck. 3.
Mitford to Newbiggin.

to Wooler

Tranwell

Common

Whalton Road

St Mary's

Abbey Park

Mitford

Castle

Fulbeck

MORPETH

Hebron

Cockle Park

Tritlington

New Opencast Site

County Hall

Station

East Mill

Viaduct

River Wansbeck

Pegswood

Longhirst Hall

Longhirst

Butterwell Opencast

Ulgham

Stobswood

Widdrington Station

Widdrington

Hepscott

Bothal Church

Bothal Castle

Conegarth

Station

Old Moor

Linton

Guide Post

Sheepwash

Ashington

East Moor

Ellington

Alcan Aluminium Works

Lynemouth

West Sleekburn

Station

Hirst

North Station

Mining Museum

Woodhorn

Newbiggin

Beacon Point

Cresswell

Cambois

Mouth of the Wansbeck

Newbiggin Bay